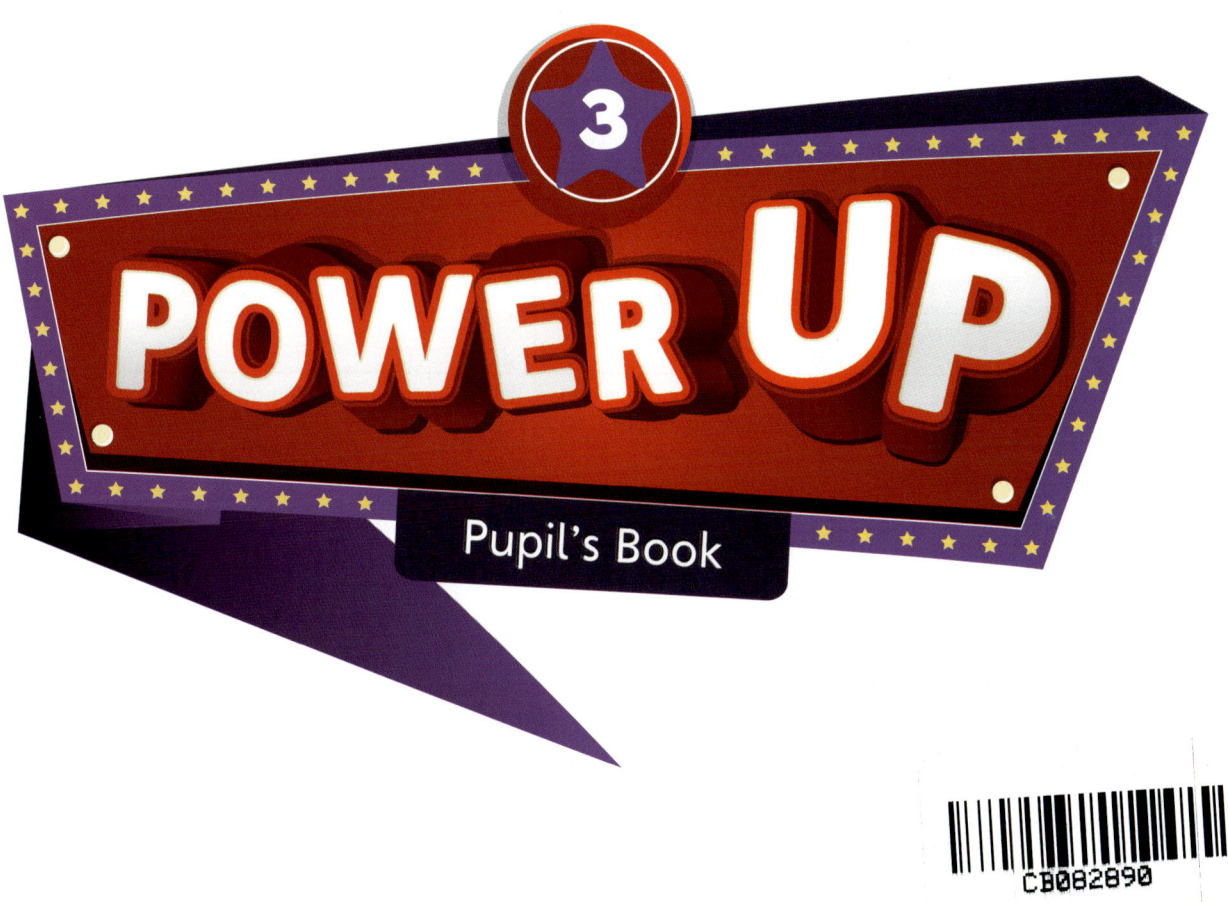

Caroline Nixon & Michael Tomlinson

Map of the book

	Vocabulary	Grammar	Cross-curricular	Literature	Assessment
Welcome to Diversicus Page 4	Main character names Greetings and introductions	Language review Questions and answers Greetings			
1 Practice time Mission: Plan a week in the life of a circus artist Page 6	Telling the time Activity verbs Sounds and spelling: numbers	Review: question words *how, what, when, where, which, who, why* was/were + could *I could hop on one leg when I was four. I couldn't skip.*	Balancing act Learn about balance and coordination A Russian Olympic athlete	The circus child A real-life story Social and emotional skill: perseverance	A1 Movers Reading and Writing Part 6
2 What's for breakfast? Mission: Become a restaurant owner Page 18	Food and drink Past simple irregular verbs Sounds and spelling: *c* spelling for 's' and 'k' sound	Defining relative clauses *It's the place where I studied. Can you see the woman who is cooking in the kitchen? They're the mountains which I climbed with my father.* Past simple + with/when *When we finished lunch we went to the funfair.*	Food, glorious food Learn about food and nutrition Breakfast in China and around the world	The old man and the small fish A real-life story Social and emotional skill: showing respect for decisions of others	A1 Movers Listening Part 5
3 A healthy body Mission: Become a health expert Page 30	Parts of the body Health problems Sounds and spelling: *kn* and *n* spelling for 'n' sound	Review of comparative and superlative adjectives, as … as *I'm not as strong as you. Jenny is taller than you. Ivan is the strongest man here.* want/need + infinitive *I want to go to the party. You need to drink. I don't want to drink.*	Work your body Learn about bones and joints Yoga in Indonesia	Too-too-moo and the Komodo dragon A fantasy play script Social and emotional skill: showing empathy for others	A1 Movers Reading and Writing Part 4
Review Units 1–3					
4 Fun in the jungle Mission: Create a jungle adventure park Page 44	Natural features Past simple verbs Sounds and spelling: *l, ll* and *le* spelling for 'l' sound	Adverbs *well, badly, loudly, quietly, quickly, slowly, carefully, beautifully, hard, fast* Comparative adverbs *Elephants can move faster than snakes. Monkeys can climb better than tigers. Bears can run more quickly than monkeys.*	From the roots to the flower Learn about plants and how they grow Carnivorous plants in India and around the world	The story of Rama and Sita An Indian myth Social and emotional skill: helping others	A1 Movers Reading and Writing Part 5

		Vocabulary	Grammar	Cross-curricular	Literature	Assessment
5	**Behind the scenes** Mission: Prepare a performance Page 56	Describing clothes Materials **Sounds and spelling:** -igh and i-e spelling	*be made of* What's it made of? It's made of gold. What are the wings made of? They're made of paper. *shall, could* and *let's* for suggestions Shall we design some props? Let's design the sea. We could use blue paper.	*Materials and properties* Learn about the properties of different materials Greek masks	*The myth of Icarus* A Greek myth Social and emotional skill: Listening to others	A2 Flyers Speaking Part 3
6	**Classroom stars** Mission: Have a school prize-giving ceremony Page 68	School subjects Extension of school vocabulary **Sounds and spelling:** *f* and *ph* spelling for 'f' sound	*should/shouldn't* You should listen to your teacher. You shouldn't talk when your teacher's giving the lesson. Should you copy in exams? No, you shouldn't. *be good at* + **noun/gerund** I'm good at maths. Are you good at sport? I'm not very good at drawing.	*Where are we?* Learn about maps and symbols Cappadocia in Turkey	*The project* A narration and poem Social and emotional skill: team work and respecting the ideas of others	A2 Flyers Listening Part 1
		Review Units 4–6				
7	**When I grow up …** Mission: Choose your dream job Page 82	Jobs Personality adjectives **Sounds and spelling:** -er, -ar and -or endings	*when* and *if* clauses (zero conditionals) When you dance, you look in the mirror. If you win, you get a big prize. If William wins, he wants to buy a fantastic new camera. *look like, be like* What does your grandad look like? He's very tall and he's got short, grey hair. What's your uncle like? He's very friendly.	*Time detectives* Learn about archaeology The Altamira Caves in Spain	*Don Quixote, Sancho and the windmills* An adventure play script Social and emotional skill: responding appropriately to other people's emotional state	A2 Flyers Reading and Writing Part 1
8	**City break** Mission: Create a guide to a town Page 94	Directions Places in town **Sounds and spelling:** revision of the 'th' sound	*Future with be going to* I'm going to take my umbrella. It isn't going to rain. What are we going to see first? *Prepositions of movement* across, into, out of, over, past, round, through	*Home, sweet home* Learn about cities, towns and villages New York City	*The road to Hope* A poem Social and emotional skill: managing own emotions	A2 Flyers Speaking Part 1
9	**Let's travel!** Mission: Organise a summer camp Page 106	Adjectives On holiday **Sounds and spelling:** *ge* spelling for 'j' sound	*before, after, when* clauses Rose got really wet before I gave her my umbrella. He ran really fast when Fred came out of the trees. After we met Grandma's sister in China, we ate the fantastic noodles. *-ed/-ing* adjective endings excited/exciting interested/interesting	*North, south, east and west* Learn about what to take on a hiking trip A hiking trip in Mexico	*The story of Popocatepetl and Iztaccihuatl* A narration and legend Social and emotional skill: showing respect for other cultures	A2 Flyers Reading and Writing Part 7
		Review Units 7–9				
		Grammar reference page 120				

Welcome to Diversicus

1  Listen. What is Diversicus?

The Friendly family are going on tour with Diversicus. Today is their first day.

Mr Friendly — Mrs Friendly — Ivan — Rose — Jim — Jenny

2 Who says it? Say the name.

3 Play the game. Ask and answer.

Who's got purple hair? — Rose.

What's the name of the circus? — Diversicus.

Greetings and introductions

4 Act out the story.

Story: Questions and answers

Practice time

 **Watch the video. Ask and answer.**

What are your hobbies?
Do you practise your hobbies every day?

mission — Plan a week in the life of a circus artist

In this unit I will:

① Prepare a weekly schedule.
② Add practice time to the schedule.
③ Add a warm-up activity to the schedule.
★ Present a schedule to the class.

Vocabulary 1

1 🎧 1.05 **Listen. Then say the letter.**

Diversicus is in Russia. This morning, Mr Friendly and Rose are talking about meals and meal times.

 a — half past twelve

 e — seven o'clock

 b — midnight

 f — half past six

 c — half past eight

 g — eight o'clock

 d — half past nine

 h — midday

2 **What time is it? Ask and answer.**

What time is it?

It's half past twelve.

3  **Ask and answer.**

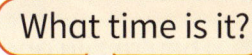

breakfast   a snack   lunch   dinner   wake up   go to bed

What time do you have breakfast?

I have breakfast at half past seven.

Telling the time

1 Listen and say *yes* or *no*.

Language practice 1

1 Describe the picture. What are they doing?

2 Read. Answer the questions.

Diversicus is a circus. There are acrobats and clowns, but there aren't any animals. The acrobats get up at half past six and they have breakfast early because they start practising at nine o'clock. Acrobats have to climb, run and jump. The strong acrobats catch the others in the air. It's very exciting. Their job is beautiful, but it's dangerous, too.

1 What is Diversicus?
2 What time do the acrobats get up?
3 Why do they have breakfast early?
4 What time do they start practising?
5 Which acrobats catch the others in the air?

 **Grammar spotlight**

Which country are we in? We're in **Russia**.
Why are you running? **Because** school starts in ten minutes.
What time do they have lunch? They have lunch at **half past twelve**.

3 Imagine you meet an acrobat from Diversicus. What do you want to know about him/her? Write three questions.

Prepare your schedule.

- Choose which circus artist you'd like to be.
- Work with a partner.
- Ask and answer to complete your partner's weekly schedule.

What time do you have breakfast?   I have breakfast at eight o'clock.
What time do you go to bed on Mondays?   At nine o'clock.

Activity Book page 6

Review question words   9

Vocabulary 2 and song

1  **Listen and do the actions. Then sing the song.**

catch

Hop, skip and dance, climb, climb, climb.
Jump to your places, it's practice time.

Dress up, dress up. Put your costumes on.
We haven't got time, we haven't got long.

Hello, kids! Are you in or out?
You must be quiet, you mustn't shout!

Ivan, don't laugh. Stand in your place.
You must catch Marc with a smile on your face.

Marc, catch Lily! Hold her legs!
She mustn't fall into the net.

Chorus

dance

shout

laugh

dress up

jump

hop

skip

climb

2 Describe the picture in Activity 1 to a partner. Use the words in the picture.

The people in purple clothes are dancing.

Let's talk about parties. Do you like dressing up for parties? What clothes do you wear?

3 Write three sentences about the picture.

Two acrobats are dressing up.

Activity verbs

Language practice 2

1  **Listen and match Daisy and Peter to a picture.**

a  b  c

Daisy

Peter

⭐ 🎧 1.12 Grammar spotlight

I **could hop** on one leg when I **was** four. I **couldn't skip**.

2 Think about when you were four. Write three sentences about what you could and couldn't do.

3 Ask and answer.

ride a bike   swim   climb trees   play the guitar   ride a skateboard
skate   sing   dance   hop   skip   cook

> Could you ride a bike when you were three?

> No, I couldn't.

_____
_____
_____

 STAGE 2

Add a practice time to the schedule.
- Ask your partner about when they practise.
- Add this information to their weekly schedule.

> When do you do practise?

> I practise on Tuesdays at five o'clock. I jump and skip.

My mission diary
Activity Book page 6

Cross-curricular

Balancing act

1  Watch the video.

2  Listen and read. Answer the question.

Can you ride a bike? Do you like ice skating or doing gymnastics? When you do these activities what helps you not to fall all the time? It's your sense of balance. Your brain controls your sense of balance. The brain is a very complicated organ. Different parts control different things. The cerebellum is the part of the brain that controls balance. Without this, it would be difficult to walk or even stand up.

Which other activities need a sense of balance?

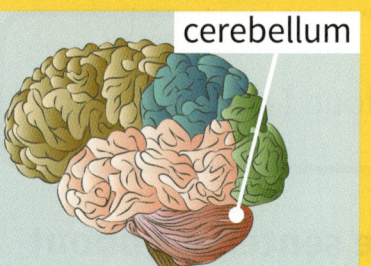

3 Look at the pictures. Which activities need balance?

1

2

3

4

4 Read and try the activities.

Test your balance. Try these activities.

 Tightrope walking.

Place a long piece of string on the floor in a straight line. Walk along the string to the end. Try it with your eyes closed, or try going backwards!

 Who's the tallest?

Work with a partner. Put one paper plate at a time onto your partner's head. Who can keep the most paper plates on their head?

Learn about balance and coordination

Culture

5  **Listen and read the text about a Russian athlete. Answer the question.**
What new move did Olga Korbut perform in 1972? _____

Olga Korbut

One sport that needs a really good sense of balance is gymnastics. And who is the queen of balance? Russian Olympic gymnast, Olga Korbut!

Olga Korbut was born in 1955 in Grodno. At the time Grodno was part of the USSR (the Soviet Union).

She studied in a school that had a special programme for sports people. She began to train for the Olympic team.

At the Olympic Games in 1972, Olga was 17 years old and the youngest member of the team. She was also very small, only 1.5 metres tall, but she was very strong. Her routines were fast and exciting and she was everyone's favourite gymnast.

Olga Korbut won four gold medals and two silver medals for the USSR in the 1972 and 1976 Olympics. In 1972, she performed new moves including the Korbut Flip. They don't do this move in competitions now because people think it is too dangerous!

It is still exciting to watch Olga Korbut's routines, but don't forget that she had to train for many hours every day to become a top gymnast. Would you like to be a gymnast?

6 Read the text again. Complete the mind map.

- Olga Korbut
- born ____
- ____ years old in the 1972 Olympics
- small but very ____
- very ____ and ____ routines
- won ____ gold medals and ____ silver medals
- invented a move called ____
- helped make ____ an exciting sport to watch

mission STAGE 3

Add a warm-up routine to your schedule.
- Work in groups.
- Think of a warm-up activity to do for your practice.
- Decide where to put it in your schedule.

My mission diary
Activity Book page 6

Learn about a Russian Olympic athlete 13

Literature

1 **Look at the pictures. Answer the questions.**
1. Would you like to be part of a circus? Why? Why not?
2. How old do you think the girl in the circus is?

THE CIRCUS CHILD

Can you imagine being in a circus? Travelling all over the world, playing with clowns, flying through the air on a trapeze, or jumping on trampolines all day? No? Well, let me tell you about it.

My name is Anastasia. I was born in the circus. My parents are Russian acrobats with *Captain Adventure's Travelling Circus* and my dream was always to be just like them and perform on stage.

Every day I wanted to ask Dad when I could go on stage with him. But I was afraid to. I didn't know if I was ready.

In the mornings I had classes with a teacher online. They started at nine o'clock. My parents said I had to do well at school. In the afternoons I practised acrobatics with my dad for hours. We practised until dinner at half past seven.

Text type: A real-life story

My dad helped me improve and learn new moves. 'Let's try a backflip,' he said one day, ready to catch me if I fell. I couldn't do backflips then, but I can now.

'Great! Again! Fantastic! Again!' he told me. I practised a lot. I really wanted to do it.

After training, my friend Yuri usually came over to give me support.
'Soon,' he always said, and hugged me.

I practised really hard every day for years, then last month it finally happened. Dad said, 'I think you are ready to go on stage now. How about Saturday?'
'Really?' I shouted and jumped up and down.

Immediately, I ran to tell Yuri the good news. 'I told you!' he laughed. 'You practised a lot, and practice makes perfect.'

And that was how my dream came true. Now I perform in the circus every week.

2 **Answer the questions.**
1. What does Anastasia do every day? Why does she do this?
2. How did Anastasia feel at the beginning of the story? How does she feel now?
3. What do you practise every day? Why?

A1 Movers

1 Talk about the picture and point.

> She's got a black hat.

> He's riding a bike.

2 Look at the picture and choose the correct word.

1. The clown with the toy plane is *walking* / *skipping* / *dancing*.
2. One hat is black and one hat is *yellow* / *pink* / *green*.
3. One of the children has got a *kitten* / *rabbit* / *penguin*.

3 Look at the picture and complete the sentences.

1. What is the boy doing? He's _____
2. The small clown is _____
3. The man in the white shirt is _____

4 Say two more things about the picture.

> I like this circus.

> The clowns are funny.

Write 2 different sentences about the picture.

Preparation for Reading and Writing Part 6

Review

mission in action!

Present a schedule to the class.

My mission diary
Activity Book page 6

★ In your groups, choose a schedule.

★ Present the schedule to the class.

This is our schedule. On weekdays, we wake up at eight o'clock. We study at ten o'clock. We do our warm-up at three o'clock. We practise jumping at five o'clock.

★ Perform your warm-up activity.

Can you remember?

1. What time do the circus artists have breakfast on Mondays?
2. Who is Marc?
3. Why does Ivan eat a lot?
4. What couldn't Peter do when he was four?
5. Name three activities that need a sense of balance.
6. What couldn't Anastasia do that she can do now?

2 What's for breakfast?

1  **Watch the video. Ask and answer.**

What time do you usually eat breakfast?
What do you usually eat?

mission Become a restaurant owner

In this unit I will:

1. Create a restaurant.
2. Talk about restaurants with a partner.
3. Create a restaurant menu.
★ Write a review about a restaurant.

Vocabulary 1

1 🎧 1.16 **Listen. What do Rose and Ivan like for breakfast?**

Diversicus is in China. Today, Mr Friendly, Ivan and the children are in the supermarket, shopping for food.

tea
cup
coffee
milkshake
glass
cereal
noodles
sauce
pancake
strawberries
yoghurt

2 🎧 1.17 ▶ **Say the chant.**

3 **Match. Then offer your partner food and drink.**

1 a glass of
2 a cup of
3 a bottle of
4 a bowl of

a coffee
b chocolate sauce
c cereal
d milkshake

milk   noodles   water
soup   coffee   lemonade
pasta   tea   salad   rice

Would you like a glass of milk?   Yes, please.

Food and drink   19

1 Listen. Who says it?

Story: Defining relative clauses in context

Language practice 1

1 Describe the picture. What are they doing?

2  **Read and check. Choose the words to complete the text.**

Look at these children ¹who are climbing up the mountain. They're on the Great Wall of China. It's a wall ² ___ people built many years ago. It's famous because it's the ³ ___ wall in the world. The Great Wall is a beautiful place ⁴ ___ people enjoy walking and ⁵ ___ photos. Would you like to ⁶ ___ on the Great Wall?

1	who	which	where
2	who	which	where
3	longest	fastest	smallest

4	who	which	where
5	doing	making	taking
6	walk	walked	walking

⭐ 🎧 1.20 Grammar spotlight

It's the place **where** I studied.

Can you see the woman **who** is cooking in the kitchen?

They're the mountains **which** I climbed with my father.

3 Play the guessing game.

It's the thing which we use to take photos. — A camera.

 **STAGE 1**

Create a restaurant.

- Choose a name and a description for your restaurant.
- Prepare a restaurant sign.
- In groups, talk about your restaurants.

My restaurant's called *Happy Noodle*. It's a Chinese restaurant where you can eat noodles for breakfast.

My mission diary

Activity Book page 18

Defining relative clauses

Vocabulary 2 and song

1 🎧 1.21 ▶ **Listen and match the words to the pictures. Then sing the song.**

Yesterday we **drove** to town.
We saw the place where May grew up.
She told us all about her school,
And the teacher who taught her there.

Oh, we **got dressed up**.
Oh, we had a great day.
Oh, we **wrote** this song.
Oh, we took some photos of it all.

Yesterday we saw May's sister.
She **gave** us all a bowl of noodles.
After lunch we **climbed** the Great Wall,
Which they built years before.

Oh, we got dressed up.
Oh, we had a great day.
Oh, we wrote this song.
Oh, we took some photos.

Oh, we got dressed up.
Oh, we had a great day.
Oh, we wrote this song.
Oh, we took some photos of it all.
We had a great day.

2 **Find the past simple form of these verbs in the song.**

> see   write   tell   build   take   drive   teach   give   have   grow   get   climb

3 **Ask and answer about the song.**

- Did they drive to the beach?
- No, they didn't. They drove to the town.
- Did they see the place where May grew up?
- Yes, they did.
- What did you do yesterday afternoon?

Past simple irregular verbs

Language practice 2

1  **Listen. What did Jack like best?**

a

b

c

⭐ 🎧 1.24 Grammar spotlight

When we **finished** lunch we **went** to the funfair.
When the bus **arrived** we all **got** on it.
We **were** sad **when** the bus **came** to take us home.

2 Ask and answer.

Questions:
arrive at school   finish school   get home from school
finish breakfast/lunch/dinner   finish your homework

Answers:
play   study   watch TV   go to school   do my homework
read   clean my teeth   listen to music

> What did you do when you finished breakfast yesterday?

> When I finished breakfast yesterday, I cleaned my teeth.

3 What did you do yesterday? Write three sentences with *when*.

_____
_____
_____

mission STAGE 2

Talk about restaurants with a partner.

• Talk about restaurants that you like and why you like them with a partner.

> When my family and I went to Mallorca, we went to a restaurant by the sea. I'd like my restaurant to be near the sea.

My mission diary
Activity Book page 18

Past simple with *when*

Cross-curricular

Food, glorious food

1  Watch the video.

2  Listen and read. What are the five main food groups?

We know that we need food to stay alive, and that it can be delicious! But we also know that we need to eat different types of food and the right amounts to stay healthy. There are five main food groups:

3 Match these foods to the groups in Activity 2.

a  b  c  d  e

4  Think of two breakfast foods for each food group.

> Carbohydrates and fibre – cereal and …

5 How healthy are your breakfast foods in Activity 4? Give each a score out of five.

1 = very unhealthy
5 = very healthy

> I think that cereal is 3. It's sometimes healthy and sometimes unhealthy when it's got a lot of sugar.

Learn about food and nutrition

Culture

6  Look at the breakfasts. Where do you think they are from? Listen and check.

7  Listen and read. Where is this breakfast from?

People often have breakfast at around seven o'clock in China because children usually go to school before eight o'clock. People often buy breakfast from a street stall and they eat it as they travel to work or school. China is a very large country and the breakfasts are different in different cities. The most popular breakfast is soya milk with youtiao. Youtiao are like long fried doughnuts. People dip them into the soya milk. Other people prefer rice noodles or buns with meat.

8  Talk to a partner about your breakfast.

I usually have ... for breakfast.

My favourite breakfast is ...

 STAGE 3

Create a restaurant menu.
- Think of some healthy food to include in your menu.
- Create and design your menu.

Activity Book page 18

Learn about breakfasts in China and around the world

Literature

1 Look at the pictures. Describe the people in the story.

🎧 1.28 The old man and the small fish

My name is Ching-Yun. I am an old man. I live in a village near the Huangshan Mountain. My granddaughter calls me 'The Happiest Man in China'.

Every day my granddaughter comes to visit me before she goes to school. Her name is Wen. She is eight years old. Wen makes breakfast for me. I have the same thing every morning – noodles and a cup of green tea. After breakfast, I tell Wen the old stories my grandpa told me when I was a boy.

It was cold that morning. Wen arrived early.
'Yéye,' she said, 'do you want something different for breakfast today – perhaps some rice or some bread?'
I said, 'No, thank you, Wen. I'm very happy with my noodles and my tea.'
'Why do you have the same thing for breakfast every day, Yéye?' Wen asked me.
I finished my breakfast and then I told Wen the story of 'The small fish which swam in the same part of the lake'.

Text type: A real-life story

There was once a small fish, and every day the small fish swam in the same part of the lake. Its friends didn't understand. They said, 'Come with us to a new part of the lake, small fish.'
But the small fish said, 'No, thank you. I'm happy here.'

One morning, the friends of the small fish didn't go to a new part of the lake. 'Why didn't you swim to a new part of the lake today?' said the small fish.

'We know every part of the lake now,' the friends of the small fish said, happily. 'But this part is still the best, so we're staying here with you.'

The next morning, Wen made me noodles and green tea. This time, she didn't ask me if I wanted something different for my breakfast.

2 **Read and discuss with a partner. Are your answers the same or different?**

1 Why do you think Wen's grandfather doesn't want to change what he has for breakfast?

2 Do you think it's better to always do the same thing (like Wen's grandfather) or always try something different? Why?

Social and emotional skills: Showing respect for decisions of others

A1 Movers

1 🎧 1.29 **Listen. Are the pictures correct? Say *yes* or *no*.**

2 🎧 1.30 **Look at the picture in Activity 3. Listen and finish the sentences.**

> The woman is between the cupboard and the man.

3 🎧 1.31 **Listen and find the things to colour and the place to write the word. There is one example.**

fruit

Listen carefully for prepositions and write the word in the correct place!

Preparation for Listening Part 5

Review

mission in action!

Write a review about a restaurant.

★ Talk to a friend about the restaurant which you went to.

Which restaurant did you go to?

I went to the Chinese restaurant. It was great!

My mission diary
Activity Book page 18

★ Write a review about the restaurant.

This restaurant was good because …
I really liked …
I didn't like … as much because …

Can you remember?

1. What's the man in the supermarket in China making?
2. Which places did May take Ivan and the children to see when they went to her town?
3. What did Jim, Jenny and their friends do after lunch?
4. Name three food items in the food group 'dairy'.
5. Where do people eat 'youtiao' for breakfast?
6. What did Wen's grandfather always have for breakfast?

3 A healthy body

 **Watch the video. Ask and answer.**

What do you do to stay healthy?
Why's it important to exercise and eat healthily?

mission: Become a health expert

In this unit I will:
1. Create a health plan.
2. Visit the doctor.
3. Add some healing tips to my health plan.
★ Make a health advice poster.

Vocabulary 1

1  **Listen. How did Ivan cut his finger?**

Diversicus is in Indonesia. This morning Ivan is doing exercise on the beach. The children are watching him.

shoulder · neck · finger · stomach · bandage · knee · toe · elbow · back

2  **Say the chant.**

3  **Listen and say *yes* or *no*.**

4  **Write two sentences about the picture.**

Parts of the body 31

Language practice 1

3

1 Look at the picture. Which part of their body do you think is the strongest?

2  Choose the words to complete the text.

A human tower is one of the ¹*exciting* / *most exciting* things to see, but it's one of the ²*most* / *more* dangerous, too. Look at these three people. The person at the bottom has to be the ³*stronger* / *strongest*. The person in the middle isn't as ⁴*biggest* / *big* as the person at the bottom, but she's ⁵*stronger* / *strong* than the person at the top. The person at the top is ⁶*small* / *smaller* and ⁷*thinner* / *thinnest* than the other two people. Her job isn't ⁸*easier* / *easy* than theirs; it's as difficult ⁹*as* / *than* theirs and sometimes it's ¹⁰*more* / *most* dangerous. Would you like to try it?

🎧 1.37 **Grammar spotlight**

| I'm not **as** strong **as** you. | Jenny is **taller than** you. | Ivan is **the strongest** man here. |

3 Make sentences about your family. Use these words.

tall   strong   big   clever   funny   careful   boring   interesting   loud   quiet

My grandma isn't as tall as my dad.

My sister's funnier than my brother.

I'm the loudest person in my family.

 **STAGE 1**

Create a health plan.
- Work with a partner. Choose three parts of the body.
- Think of ways to keep these parts of the body healthy and fit.
- Add these ideas to your health plan.

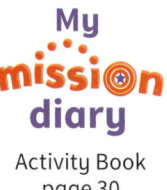
Activity Book page 30

Review of comparative and superlative adjectives, *as … as*

1 1.38 Listen and match the names to the words. Then sing the song.

They're all sick,
They're all ill.
They're all ill,
They're all sick.
Doctor, Doctor,
Please be quick!

What's the problem?
What's the matter?
What's the problem?
What's the matter?

He's got a **cough**
And a **temperature**,
She's got a **sore throat**
And a **cold**.

Chorus

My back hurts.
I've got a **backache**.
My stomach hurts.
Ooh **stomach-ache**.

Chorus

38°
Claire
Doctor
Charlie
Paul
Sally

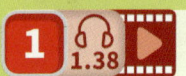

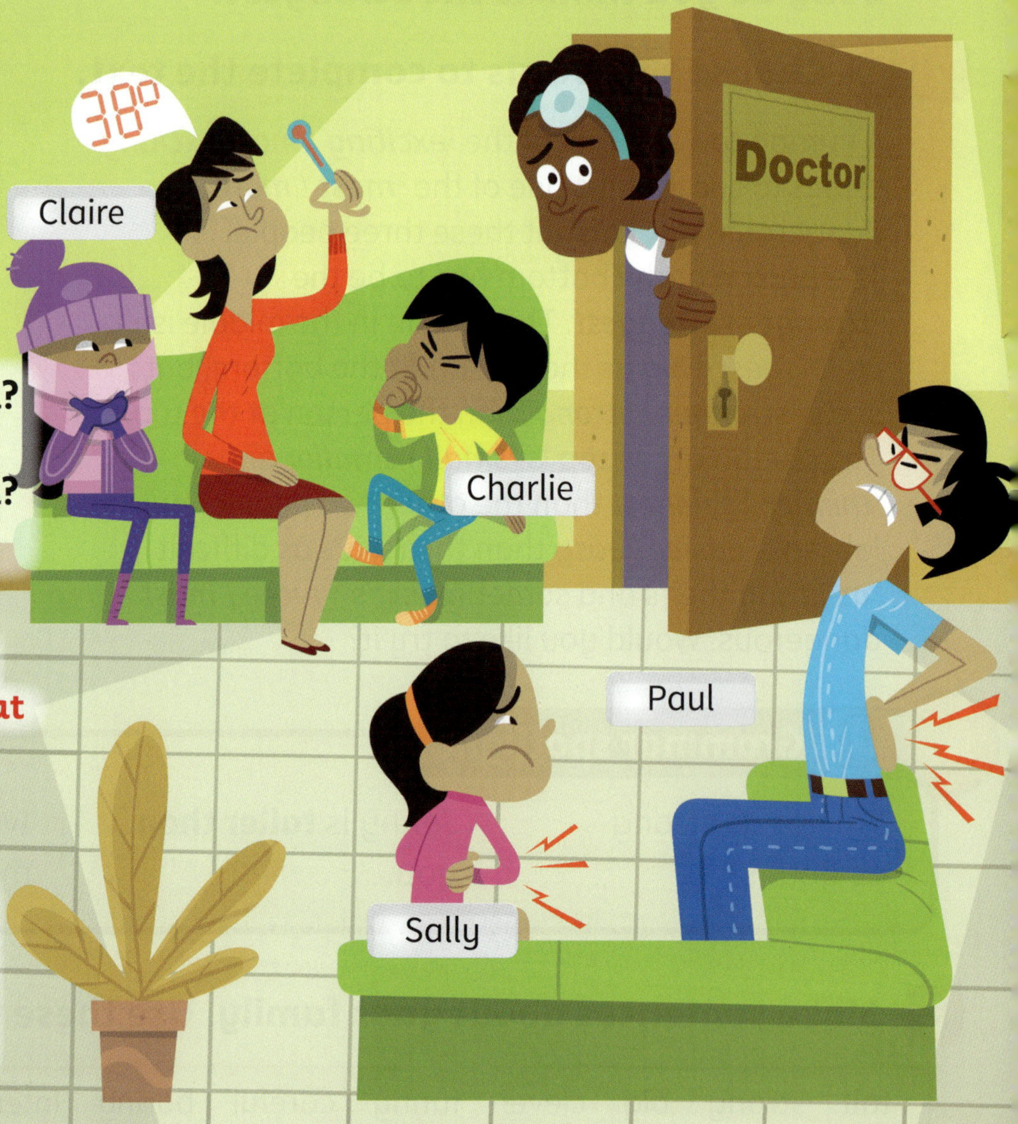

2 Play the guessing game. Ask and answer.

Does your head hurt? — No, it doesn't.

Does your back hurt? — Yes, it does.

You've got backache. — Yes, that's right.

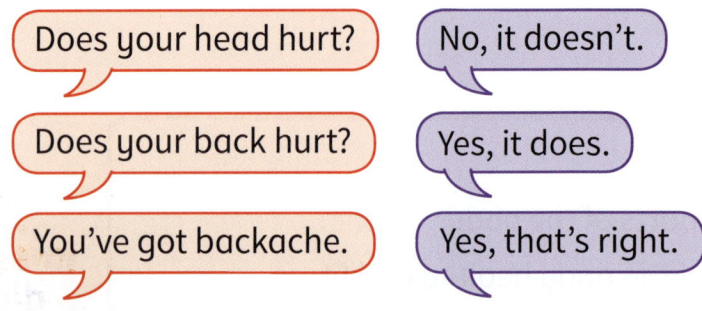

What do you do
when you feel ill?

3 1.40 Listen. Write the words.

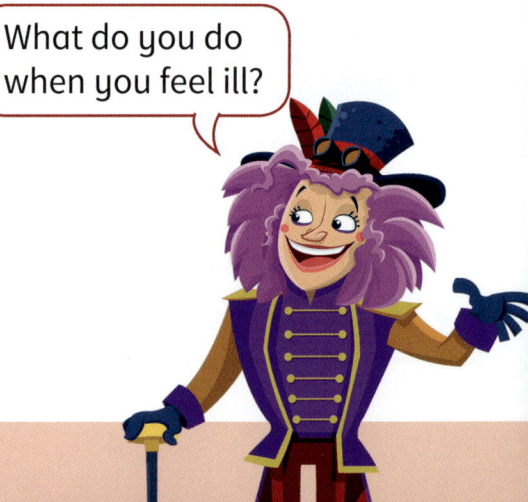

Language practice 2

1  **Listen. What does Vicky need to do?**

_____

 **Grammar spotlight**

I **want to go** to the party.
You **need to drink**.
I **don't want to drink**.

2  **Write questions and answers with *but*.**

| sing   eat some cake   play football   go to a party   play the guitar   study |

| a stomach-ache   a sore throat   ill   fingers hurt   a headache   a temperature |

> What's the matter?
> I want to play football after school, but I've got a headache.
> You need to sit down, but you can watch the game.

3  **What do you want to do? What do you need to do? Write two sentences for each question.**

> I want to go to the cinema. I need to do my homework.

 **STAGE 2**

Visit the doctor.

- Work with a partner. One person is a doctor and the other person is a patient.
- Patient: Tell the doctor what's wrong with you.
- Doctor: Give the patient some advice.

> What's the matter?

> I want to go to the football match, but I've got a temperature.

> You need to stay at home and rest.

- Swap roles. Then add the advice to your health plan.

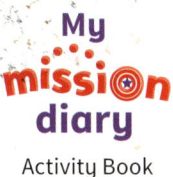

My mission diary
Activity Book page 30

want/need + infinitive

Cross-curricular

Work your body

1  **Watch the video. Then read the text.**

> Did you know there are over 200 bones in our bodies? Bones shape our body and hold us together. Between each bone we have a joint. Joints help us to move. It's important to protect our bones and joints, especially when we're doing sports and other dangerous activities.

2 Match the parts of the body to the bones and joints.

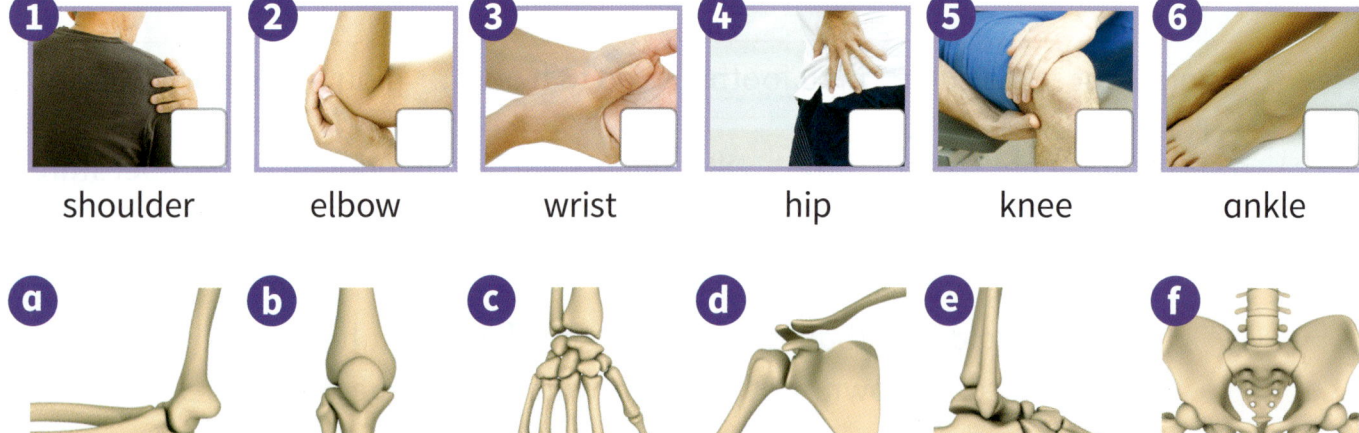

1. shoulder
2. elbow
3. wrist
4. hip
5. knee
6. ankle

a b c d e f

3 What activities are the joints in Activity 2 important for? Discuss with a partner.

> The shoulder is important for throwing and carrying things, …

4 Look and match the sports to the protective equipment. Which parts of the body do they protect?

skiing ☐   horse riding ☐   skating ☐   swimming ☐   riding a bike ☐

a helmet

b swimming goggles

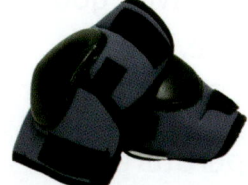
c knee and elbow pads

d boots

e goggles

Learn about bones and joints

Culture

3

5 What activities can make our body and joints stronger? Discuss with a partner.

6 🎧 1.43 Listen and read. Follow the instructions with a partner.

YOGA

Welcome to Bali, Indonesia!
On this beautiful island, yoga is very important. The people here use it to exercise and stay healthy. It's a great way to stretch your body and make your joints and muscles strong. At our centre, you can do yoga in our relaxing rooms, in the sunny garden, or on the beach! Here are a few moves we practise. Why don't you try them?

TREE POSE
Stand on one leg. Bend the other knee and put your foot on your other leg. Put your hands together above your head. Hold the position for ten seconds and breathe.

FLOWER POSE
Sit on the floor. Bend your legs. Put one foot on top of the other. Put your hands on your knees and close your eyes. Hold the position for ten seconds and breathe.

CHILD'S POSE
Kneel on the floor and sit back on your feet. Bring your head down to rest on the floor. Stretch your arms out in front of you. Hold the position for ten seconds and breathe.

7 Read and write.

This pose is called the warrior pose. Write instructions to explain how to do this pose. Use the words in the box. Then test your instructions on a partner.

stand   turn   raise   bend   stretch

mission STAGE 3

Add some healing tips to your health plan.
- With your partner, think about some ways to stay healthy.

  > Breathe slowly to keep calm.

  > Get lots of rest to have energy the next day.

- Add these ideas to your health plan.

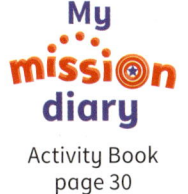

My mission diary
Activity Book page 30

Learn about yoga in Indonesia

Literature

1 **Read these words. Which of them can you find in the pictures?**

dragon   porridge   poor   angry   girl   breakfast   roar   firewood

🎧 1.44 TOO-TOO-MOO AND THE KOMODO DRAGON

SCENE ONE

Narrator: This is a story from Indonesia about Too-too-moo and the Komodo dragon.
Mother: Breakfast is ready.
Too-too-moo: Oh no. Rice again!
Mother: We're poor. And remember, the dragon gets porridge. I make it for him every day. He eats all of our porridge!
Too-too-moo: I know he eats a lot, but he's the biggest dragon in the world! He's my friend.
Mother: He's a wild animal. You need to be careful!
Narrator: And so Mother left to collect firewood to sell in the market.

SCENE TWO

Narrator: There was a knock on the door!
Too-too-moo: That's the dragon. He knocks on the door louder every day.
Dragon: Too-too-moo! Where are you? I'm hungry, and I need my porridge.
Narrator: Too-too-moo gave the dragon his breakfast. The dragon roared, and then he walked away with the porridge.

Text type: A fantasy play script

SCENE THREE

Narrator: The weather was hot. Nobody wanted firewood so Too-too-moo and her mother couldn't make any money. They got poorer and poorer. Soon there was no food in the little house. But still the Komodo dragon came for his porridge.

Dragon: Too-too-moo! Where are you? I'm hungry, and I need my breakfast. Open the door! I've got a stomach-ache. I can't wait any more!

Narrator: Too-too-moo opened the door.

Too-too-moo: There isn't any porridge.

Narrator: The dragon was angry. He pushed Too-too-moo. He showed his terrible teeth, and he gave a terrible roar.

Dragon: Too-too-moo, you aren't my friend any more!

SCENE FOUR

Narrator: At last the weather got colder. People bought firewood again. Too-too-moo's mother came home with rice and porridge.

Mother: I'm happy that greedy dragon doesn't come here now. There is more food for us!

Too-too-moo: He wasn't greedy, Mother. He was hungry.

Mother: He's dangerous! He needs to stay in the forest where he belongs.

Narrator: The dragon never came to the little house again. But Too-too-moo often left a bowl of porridge in the forest for his breakfast.

2 Why do you think Too-too-moo gives the dragon breakfast at the end?

3 Remember and write.

Close your book. Work in groups. Write a simple summary of the story. Write seven sentences. Share your sentences with the class.

4 Act out the play.

Social and emotional skills: Showing empathy for others

A1 Movers

1 Read and put the words in the table.

~~hands~~   a bus   jump   a horse
better   older   children   hurt
needs   long   know   a sport

Noun (s.)	Noun (pl.)	Adjective	Verb
	hands		

2 Choose the correct option to complete the sentences.

1 I had a headache this morning, but it *don't* / *doesn't* hurt now.

2 I look after my *body* / *bodies* by exercising every day.

3 Our shoes are *between* / *in* the cupboard.

4 My mum *has* / *have* got a backache.

5 We went to *their* / *they're* house for breakfast.

6 My friend has got longer arms *then* / *than* me.

3 Look at the picture and the title. Read and find words about the picture. Choose the right words to complete the sentences.

Legs

Before they walk, young children learn to move around __on__ their hands and knees. A horse has got four legs and a spider has got eight legs. Snakes ____ got any legs but they've got long bodies!

Legs can help us to jump or ____ , for example, when we need to catch a bus. When you play a sport like football or tennis, you sometimes hurt your knee or foot. If it's very sore, don't worry ____ a doctor in a hospital can make you better.

Most people have two legs, two knees, two feet and ten toes. Did you know that there are 52 bones in our feet? Are you surprised?

	Example		
	on	in	at
1	have	haven't	had
2	ran	running	run
3	because	and	but

Copy the word you choose on the right line.

Preparation for Reading and Writing Part 4

Review

mission in action!   3

Make a health advice poster.

- ★ Work in groups. Share your health plan with your group.
- ★ Discuss the best ideas in each section.

"I think Lisa's healing tips are the best. Do you agree?"

"Yes, and I think Dan's health advice is the best."

- ★ Make a poster with some health advice for the class.

My mission diary
Activity Book page 30

Can you remember?

1. How did Ivan hurt his toe?
2. What is Puncak Jaya?
3. Who has backache in the song?
4. What does Vicky want to do? Why can't she do it?
5. What protective equipment do you need to wear when you ride a bike?
6. Why was the Komodo dragon angry with Too-too-moo?

Review — Units 1–3

1 Watch the video and do the quiz.

2 🎧 1.45 What do they need? Listen and choose.

1 a b c
2 a b c
3 a b c
4 a b c

3 Play the game with a partner. Choose a square. Your partner makes a sentence with that word and language from the box.

| highest | biggest | longest | strongest | best | clever | as … as | more exciting |

1 me	5 mountain	9 kangaroo	13 cinema
2 a shop	6 milkshake	10 dancer	14 English
3 jump	7 river	11 lake	15 my friend
4 pop star	8 restaurant	12 books	16 elephant

Number 5 – mountain.

Mount Teide is the highest mountain in Spain.

Number 15 – my friend.

I am as clever as my friend Javier.

Consolidation of units 1–3

4 Read the text and order the pictures.

Julia and Paul's busy day
WEEK 1

31 Wednesday Mercredi Mittwock Miércoles Mercoledi

8: At eight o'clock Julia and Paul woke up. At half past eight they had cereal and pancakes for breakfast.

9: At half past nine Dad told them to 'come on!'

10: At ten o'clock Mum drove them to the countryside. They saw the hospital where Mum worked.

11: At eleven o'clock they climbed trees and they took photos. They had the best time with their mum, who taught them how to build mountains of leaves. They built five!

12: At twelve o'clock their dad made them noodles and sauce for lunch.

a   b   c   d   e   f

5 Cover the text and use the pictures to retell the story.

6 Copy the table and add two activities. Ask your family and complete.

Could you hop when you were three?

No, but I could dance!

	Hop	Climb trees	?	?
Me				
?				
?				

7 Write sentences. Use the information from the table in Activity 6.

My sister couldn't hop when she was three, but she could dance.

Consolidation of units 1–3

4 Fun in the jungle

1 ▶ **Watch the video. Ask and answer.**

What do you like to do outside?
Where's your favourite natural place?

TAJ MAHAL

mission — Create a jungle adventure park

In this unit I will:

1. Design a map for a jungle adventure park.
2. Invent a jungle activity.
3. Add a nature area in the park.
★ Present the jungle adventure park to the class.

Vocabulary 1

1 🎧 2.02 **Listen. What did May and Fred make last week?**

Diversicus is in India. This afternoon Rose is talking to Fred and May about the new show for their world tour.

moon
sky
star
waterfall
jungle
plant
wave
world
island

2 🎧 2.03 ▶ **Say the chant.**

3 🎧 2.04 **Listen. Who says it? Say the name.**

Rose   Mrs Friendly   May   Fred   Pablo

Natural features   45

DIVERSICUS

1. Today, we're having our lessons in the Indian jungle. How exciting!
We mustn't talk loudly if we want to see animals hiding in the plants.
Animals? Hiding?

2. We can study birds really well here.
Yeah, and let's look hard in the trees to see some monkeys.
CRACK
What was that? Was it a bear?

3. No, only me! Can I come, too?
OK, Ivan, but we must walk slowly, carefully and quietly in the jungle.

4. The water's moving really quickly. What a fantastic waterfall!
OK, everyone. Look carefully at the plants and draw them, please.

5. This is very difficult. I can't do it. I draw really badly.
Don't worry! You can do it easily. Look, I can help you.

6. So, what's the most dangerous animal in the jungle? Is it the bear?
No, I think it's the snake.

7. Ivan! Walk slowly and carefully, please!
No, Miguel! Run quickly! Move! Fast! There's a bear behind us!

8. I worked really hard to make this costume, and it worked well because you all thought I was a real bear!

1 🎧 2.06 **Listen and complete. Use two words.**

Story: Adverbs in context

Language practice 1

4

1 Look at the pictures. Which instrument do you think they play to make the sounds?

a   b   c   d   e   f

2 🎧 2.07 How are they playing the instruments? Choose, then listen and check.

1. A waterfall: he's playing the piano *slowly / quickly* and *loudly / quietly*.
2. Bad weather at sea: he's playing the drums *slowly / fast* and *loudly / quietly*.
3. Sunny island: she's playing the guitar *loudly / quietly* and *slowly / quickly*.
4. Rain in the jungle: he's playing the piano *slowly / quickly* and *loudly / quietly*.
5. A bird in the tree: she's singing *beautifully / badly*.
6. Waves at night time: she's playing the piano *loudly / quietly* and *slowly / quickly*.

⭐ 🎧 2.08 **Grammar spotlight**

We mustn't talk loud**ly**.   Look careful**ly** at the plants.   It worked **well**.

3 Think of your family. Read and answer.

Who …   talks quietly?   eats loudly?   runs fast?   listens carefully?

mission STAGE 1

Design a map for a jungle adventure park.
- Work in groups. Choose a name for your park.
- Draw a map of the park.
- Label the natural features. Write a short description of each one.

This is the waterfall. The water is moving fast.

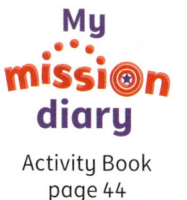

My mission diary
Activity Book page 44

Adverbs of manner | 47

Vocabulary 2 and song

1 🎧 2.09 ▶ **Listen and match. Then sing the song.**

Carefully, carefully, carefully, carefully
We flew to the jungle.
Carefully …
We drove to the beach
And we sailed on the sea.
Yes, we did …

Slowly, slowly, slowly, slowly
We fished in a river.
Slowly …
We threw our nets
And we caught some fish.
Yes, we did …

Quickly, quickly, quickly, quickly
We learnt to dance.
Quickly …
We bounced and hopped.
And we skipped and kicked.
Yes, we did …

2 **Find the past simple verbs in the song. Are they regular or irregular? Write two lists.**

3 **Play the memory game. Cover the song. Look at the pictures and say what the people did.**

Let's talk about weekends. What did you do last weekend?

48 Past simple verbs

Language practice 2

1 🎧 2.11 **Which is Peter's favourite animal? Listen, look and choose.**

a b c d e f

🎧 2.12 **Grammar spotlight**

Elephants can move **faster** than snakes.

Monkeys can climb **better** than tigers.

Bears can run **more quickly** than monkeys.

2 **Choose two animals. Make sentences with a partner.**

Animals: elephants bats tigers snakes monkeys bears

Verbs: move run jump fly swim

Adverbs: well loudly quietly quickly slowly carefully hard fast

Elephants and tigers.

Tigers can run more quickly than elephants.

mission STAGE 2

Invent a jungle activity.

- In your groups, discuss some ideas for activities to do in your jungle adventure park.

How about sailing on the lake?

Good idea, or what about fishing in the sea?

- Choose an activity and add it to your brochure.
- Write a short description and add a picture.

This activity is fishing. You sail in a boat with a guide. You fish for two hours. You can eat the fish for dinner!

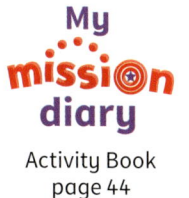

My mission diary
Activity Book page 44

Comparative adverbs

Cross-curricular

From the roots to the flower

1 🎬 **Watch the video.**

2 🎧 2.13 **Listen and read. Then answer the questions.**

> Plants are living things and grow almost everywhere – from the bottom of the sea to the highest mountain. What plants grow near you?
>
> Most plants make food using sunlight. They also need water to survive, just like us!
>
> Plants usually have three parts to them: roots, a stem and leaves. The roots take up water from the ground and the leaves take in sunlight and air around them for food. Some plants also have flowers or fruit.

1 Where do plants grow?

2 What do plants need to survive?

3 What three parts do plants usually have?

4 What other parts do plants sometimes have?

5 What's your favourite plant?

3 **Look at the diagram of the plant. Find each part in the photo.**

flower, fruit, leaves, stem, roots

4 **Draw a plant and label it. Tell your partner about your plant.**

> My favourite plant is a sunflower. This is its flower …

Learn about plants and how they grow

Culture

5 🎧 2.14 Listen and read. Then answer the questions.

Carnivorous plants

Like most other plants, carnivorous plants need sun, air and water to make their own food. But they also get extra nutrients by eating small animals! Here are two examples:

The Venus flytrap

Venus flytraps grow naturally in the USA but are used as house plants all over the world. They use their leaves to catch insects, like flies. The leaves close when an insect touches the tiny hairs that grow on them. The plant can then slowly eat the insect.

The Sundew plant

Sundew plants are found in the Indian rainforests. They can grow in soil that is underwater. Their leaves have sticky hairs and when an insect lands on the leaves, the sticky hairs trap them. Large sundew plants can trap and eat spiders.

Which plant …
1. is from India? _____
2. is from the USA? _____
3. eats flies? _____
4. sometimes eats spiders? _____
5. has got sticky hairs? _____
6. has got tiny hairs? _____

6 Create your own carnivorous plant.
Draw and colour a carnivorous plant on a sheet of paper. Make notes about where it grows, how it catches its food and what it needs to survive. Think of a name for your plant. Then present your plant to the class.

mission STAGE 3

Add a nature area to your park.
- In your groups, discuss what plants and animals you can see in your park.

  Let's have some tigers and bears.

  OK, then we need some trees with fruit for the bears to eat.

- Add this information to your brochure.

My mission diary
Activity Book page 44

Learn about carnivorous plants in India and around the world

Literature

1 Look at the pictures. What do you think the story is about? Discuss with a partner.

🎧 THE STORY OF RAMA AND SITA
2.15

Long ago a king lived in the town of Ayodhya. He had four sons.
One day he said, 'I am getting very old now and I want my oldest son Rama to be king.'
'No!' Rama's stepmother cried. '*My* son must be king!'
The King listened to his wife, and he sadly told his oldest son to leave. Rama couldn't return to Ayodhya for 14 years.

Rama and his wife, Sita, left Ayodhya. They travelled for many days until they came to a forest. 'This looks like the perfect place to live,' said Rama. For many years, they lived happily in the forest. But there was a terrible man called Ravana in the forest. He saw Sita one day and he wanted to take her. He had a plan.

One day, Sita saw a beautiful golden deer. 'Rama, catch it for me,' she said.
When Rama left to catch the deer, Ravana came to the house dressed in a costume. He caught Sita and took her back to his palace.

When Rama returned and saw that Sita wasn't there, he searched but he couldn't find her. He decided to ask Hanuman for help. Hanuman was the great leader of the monkeys. He could fly over mountains, change size and he was very strong. 'Don't worry. I can find her quickly,' he said to Rama.

Text type: An Indian myth

On her way to Ravana's palace, Sita carefully dropped her jewellery. As Hanuman flew in the sky, the pieces of jewellery were like little lights showing him the way. Soon he found Sita. She was in the garden of Ravana's palace.

Hanuman quickly told Rama where Sita was. He organised a great army of monkeys and bears. Together, they rescued her from Ravana.

Rama and Sita were happy again, and finally, after 14 years, they went back to Ayodhya. There were flowers and lanterns in the streets. The people cheered loudly and were very happy to see their real king.

In some parts of the world today, people still celebrate Rama going home.

2 **Who do you think is brave/clever/unkind/helpful in the story?**

3 **How do you think the characters feel in these parts of the story?**
- When the King tells Rama and Sita to leave Ayodhya
- When Ravana takes Sita
- When Hanuman tells Rama he found Sita
- When Rama and Sita return to Ayodhya

Social and emotional skills: Helping others

A1 Movers

A trip to the mountain

1 **Look at the first picture and the title. Describe the picture.**

2 **Look at the next two pictures and tell the story.**

a

b

3 **Read the sentences. Match them to the correct picture in Activity 2.**

1 In the evening they ate dinner outside.
2 They sang loudly after dinner.
3 Paul showed them some photos.
4 They sat in the kitchen.

4 **Read the text for the first picture in Activity 1. Then choose the correct answer to complete the sentences.**

> Vicky and Zoe's uncle lives on a mountain next to a forest. Yesterday, the girls and their parents went there by train. When they arrived it was windy.
>
> 'Hi, Paul. It's colder here than at home!' said Vicky. 'I haven't got a scarf. I don't want a sore throat!'
>
> 'Here, take my scarf,' said Paul.
>
> They played with the dog and then they all went quickly inside for lunch.

1 Vicky said the weather was _____ than at her home. (*windy / cold / colder*)
2 Paul gave Vicky _____ (*her scarf / his scarf / scarf*)

The answers can be one, two or three words.

Preparation for Reading and Writing Part 5

Review

mission in action!

4

Present your jungle adventure park to the class.

- ★ Show your brochure to the class.
- ★ Explain your jungle activity, and why it's fun.
- ★ Talk about the nature area.
- ★ As a class, vote for the best jungle adventure park.

This is our park. It's got a waterfall, a beach and a big mountain.

Our jungle activity is a fishing trip. It is an amazing experience!

Do you like tigers? Well there are lots to see in our park.

My mission diary
Activity Book page 44

Can you remember?

1. Who is afraid of waves?
2. How should Ivan walk in the jungle?
3. Where did the children in the song go fishing?
4. What can tigers do at night time?
5. Name three parts of a plant.
6. How did Rama rescue Sita?

Unit consolidation

5 Behind the scenes

1 ▶ **Watch the video. Ask and answer.**

What's your favourite play or show?
Who are the characters? What do they look like?

mission Prepare a performance

In this unit I will:

1. Design a costume.
2. Create a set and some props.
3. Make a mask.
★ Write a scene and put on a performance.

Vocabulary 1

1 🎧 2.16 **Listen. What is the name of the new show?**

Today Diversicus is in Greece. Jim and Jenny are talking to Rose about the new show.

wing
gold
silver
striped
bright
light
spotted
dark

2 🎧 2.17 ▶ **Say the chant.**

3 **Play the describing game.**

- He's wearing bright orange trousers.
- Is it Marc?
- Yes it is!

Describing clothes

DIVERSICUS

1. This show's called Icaria. It's an island in Greece. Do you like the new tree?

Yes! What's it made of?

It's made of brown and green rubber.

2. Rubber? My eraser's made of rubber.

Yes, rubber is one of the safest materials for acrobats.

3. Here are Lily's wings.

Can I put them on?

OK, but please be careful; they aren't very strong. They aren't made of rubber.

4. That's clever. The wings are made of paper. Are these the wings for the show?

No, Jim. They're only for the practice.

5. Look at that helmet. It's made of gold!

No, Jenny, it isn't. We painted it gold.

6. These are the wings for the show. What do you think they're made of?

Wow! They're made of old T-shirts!

7. We always recycle things to make the costumes. We painted the old T-shirts gold and now we have to cut them up. Would you like to help us?

8. I'd really like to help, but … it's time for me to fly.

1 Listen to the sentences and say the answers.

Story: *be made of* in context

Language practice 1

5

1 Read the text. What clothes does Robin describe?

> These are the ¹clothes for my costume. The trousers are ²____ of paper. They're ³____ purple with yellow ⁴____ . I've got yellow and purple ⁵____ shoes. They're made of ⁶____ . My helmet ⁷____ made of gold.
>
> **Robin**

🎧 2.20 Grammar spotlight

What's it **made of**?	It**'s made of** gold.
What are the wings **made of**?	The wings **are made of** paper.

2 Read Activity 1 again and choose the correct answer. Use the words in the box.

> ~~clothes~~   striped   bright   made   rubber   is   spots

3 Describe the costume in the picture.

> He's wearing a black hat. It's made of …

mission STAGE 1

Design a costume.
- Choose a character from a play, film or book.
- Design a costume for the character. Think about what it's made of.
- Write a description of your costume and what it's made of.
- In groups, talk about your costume.

> This is my design for a Peter Pan costume. He's wearing a hat. It's made of green paper …

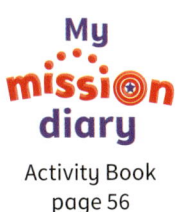

My mission diary
Activity Book page 56

be made of

Vocabulary 2 and song

1 🎧 2.21 ▶ **Listen and match the materials to the numbers. Then sing the song.**

Making, making, making,
Making all day long.
Card, metal glass,
plastic, wool and wood.

Cut them up, cut them out,
Colour in, and glue!

We make, we make,
we make, we make these things.

These scissors are made of **metal**,
This scarf is made of **wool**.
My box is made of **plastic**,
And my table's made of **wood**.

Chorus

That crown is made of brown **card**,
And I've got **silver** wings.
These balls are made of **glass**,
And I've got four **gold** rings.

Chorus

2 **Read and answer. Make two more riddles.**

1. It's made of paper. You read it. What is it?
2. It's made of wood. You sit on it. What is it?
3. It's made of wool. You use it to keep your neck warm. What is it?
4. It's made of gold. You wear it on your finger. What is it?

3 **Play the game. What is it?**

I can see something – it's made of wood. What is it?

Is it the teacher's desk?

Yes, that's right!

Look around! What are your things made of?

60 Materials

Language practice 2

1 🎧 2.23 **Listen. What are Kelly and Sophia designing?**

_____

2 🎧 2.24 **Listen again. What material do they use for each thing?**

_____

sea   sun   clouds

⭐ 🎧 2.25 **Grammar spotlight**

Shall we design some props?
Let's design the sea.
We could use blue paper.

3 **Read the situations. Share ideas with a partner. Use *Shall*, *Let's* and *We could*.**

1 You're at the cinema. What film do you want to watch?
2 You're in the playground. What game can you play?
3 It's your friend's birthday. What present do you want to buy for him/her?

Shall we watch a funny film?

Let's play hide and seek!

We could buy Julia a ring.

mission STAGE 2

Create a set and some props.
- Think of your character from Mission Stage 1. Make a group with different characters.
- In your groups, think of a set. Where are the characters?
- Think of some props and decide what materials you need to make them.
- Now make your set and props.

My mission diary
Activity Book page 56

should, *could* and *let's* for suggestions

Cross-curricular

Materials and properties

1 Watch the video.

2 🎧 2.26 Listen and read. Say the opposites.

This crown is made of gold. Gold is **heavy**.

This table is made of wood. Wood is **rigid**.

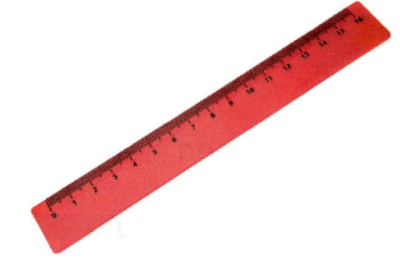

This ruler is made of plastic. Plastic is **flexible**.

This house is made of bricks. Bricks are **rough**.

This newspaper is made of paper. Paper is **light**.

This slide is made of metal. Metal is **smooth**.

The opposite of heavy is …

3 Read and say.
1. Find something flexible and something rigid in the classroom.
2. Think of something heavy and something light at home.
3. Think of something rough and something smooth outside.

4 Choose and say.

Plastic is a good material for this because it's light and rigid.

Is it a cup?

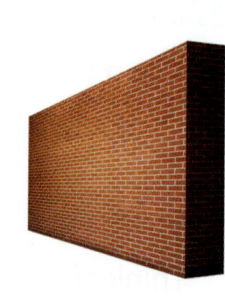

Yes it is!

Learn about the properties of different materials

Culture

5 🎧 2.27 **Listen and read. Then read the sentences and say *yes* or *no*.**

A theatre workshop

In our theatre group, we use different materials to make our costumes, props and sets. We use materials with different **properties**. Some materials are flexible and light. Some materials are rigid and strong. It's important to use materials that are safe.

We make masks with papier-mâché. It's flexible and light because it is made of paper, glue and water. You can paint the masks and decorate them with lots of different things.

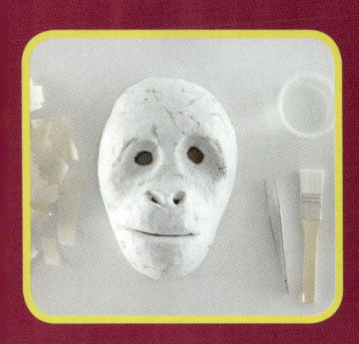

Today we're making Greek masks. Theatre was very important in Ancient Greece. Most cities had a theatre and people went there to watch comedies (funny shows) or tragedies (sad or serious shows). The actors used masks to show different emotions more clearly. Some masks were double-sided, which means they could have one face on one side and a different one on the other side. Let's make happy and sad double-sided masks!

1 All materials are flexible and soft.
2 Papier-mâché is made with paper, glue and water.
3 You can't paint papier-mâché.
4 People in Ancient Greece didn't like the theatre.
5 Tragedies were usually serious shows.
6 You can have two different emotions on double-sided masks.

mission STAGE 3

Make a mask.

Instructions
1 Cut a newspaper into strips.
2 Mix water and glue in a bowl.
3 Put the paper strips (one by one) in the bowl and cover them with the glue.
4 Put the strips on a plastic mask.
5 When it's dry, paint and decorate your mask.

- In groups, read the instructions.
- Design and then make a mask for your character.
- Tell the class about your mask.

My mask is very light. It's made of papier-mâché.

My mask is bright purple with gold stripes.

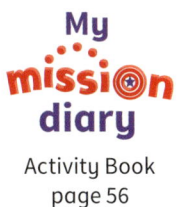

My mission diary
Activity Book page 56

Learn about Greek masks

Literature

1 Look at the pictures. What do you think the story is about? Discuss with a partner.

THE MYTH OF ICARUS

2.28

One morning on the island of Crete, Icarus and his father Daedalus were in their workshop. Daedalus was an inventor. Suddenly, King Minos arrived and he spoke to Daedalus.
'I'd like you to build me a labyrinth,' he said. 'I want to put that Minotaur inside it.' The Minotaur was a terrible monster. He had the head of a bull and the body of a man.

King Minos was pleased when he saw Daedalus's work. He put the Minotaur inside the labyrinth. Then he locked Daedalus and Icarus inside a tower. 'What are you doing?' said Daedalus. 'Well,' said the King, 'you know the secret of how to get out of the labyrinth. And I don't want anyone else to know it.'

Daedalus and his son felt sad. Days passed, then Daedalus had an idea. He collected feathers from the birds that flew to the window of the tower. Then he made wings with the feathers. He used wax from a candle to stick the feathers together.

64 Text type: A Greek myth

Daedalus told Icarus what to do. 'Follow me. Don't go too high because the sun will melt the wax in your wings. Don't go too low because the sea will make the feathers in your wings wet. Are you ready? Go!' Daedalus and Icarus jumped out of the window. They flew away from the island, and away from King Minos.

Daedalus flew in front, Icarus followed behind. Icarus loved flying. He was just like a bird! He forgot his father's words and he flew higher and higher. But as he got nearer to the sun, the wax between the feathers began to melt.

When Daedalus looked behind him, he couldn't see his son. 'Icarus!' he shouted. *'Icarus! Where are you?'* Daedalus looked down. There were feathers in the sea. Daedalus went to the nearest island. He sat and looked at the sea for a long time, and he felt sad for his son. That island is now called Icaria, and the sea around it is called the Icarian Sea.

2 Read and answer.

1. Do you like the story?
2. What is the most exciting part?
3. What is the saddest part?
4. Do you know any other Greek myths? Who are the characters? What happens?

3 Act out with a partner.

Imagine you are Icarus and Daedalus in the tower. Talk about how to escape.

> How can we get out of here?

> We could …

> OK, let's try to…

Social and emotional skills: Listening to others

A2 Flyers

1 Finish these sentences.

> I like reading / listening to stories about …

> My favourite kind of costume is …

> I don't like costumes made of …

> The best objects to make are …

> I'd like to have a … made of …

2 Look at these pictures. They tell a story. Read and say *yes* or *no*.

1. A boy is putting on a robot costume with his mum. His name is Charlie.
2. Charlie is at a competition. It's four o'clock.
3. Charlie is buying his favourite toy monster. His mum is reading a comic.
4. Charlie is standing next to two people in costumes. He's crying.
5. Charlie is the winner! He's got some DVDs and he's happy. A man is taking a photo.

> Talk about all the pictures.

3 Listen. Now you finish the story. 2.29

Preparation for Speaking Part 3

Review

mission in action!

Write a scene and put on a performance.

⭐
- Plan and write a scene in your groups
- What's the name of the show?
- Who are the characters?
- What are they doing?
- What do they say?
- Where are they?

My mission diary
Activity Book page 56

⭐ Talk about your costumes, props and masks.

My crown is made of gold paper and my mask is made of card.

⭐ Act out your scene for the class.

Can you remember?

1 Which circus artist is wearing a spotted shirt?
2 What are the practice wings made of?
3 Say something made of plastic.
4 What do Kelly and Sophia use to make the clouds?
5 Name three materials that are flexible.
6 Why did Icarus fall into the sea?

Unit consolidation 67

6 Classroom stars

1 ▶ **Watch the video. Ask and answer.**

What are your favourite subjects at school?
Why do you like these subjects?

HAGIA SOPHIA

mission Have a school prize-giving ceremony

In this unit I will:
1. Describe how to be good at a subject.
2. Find out what my classmates are good at.
3. Make a prize for each subject or activity.
4. Give prizes to my classmates.

Vocabulary 1

1 🎧 2.30 **Listen. What homework does Miguel give the children?**

Diversicus is in Turkey. This morning the children are at school with Miguel. They're in the classroom.

geography   history   sports   maths
language   music   science   IT   art

2 🎧 2.31 ▶ **Say the chant.**

3 📝 **Write your school timetable. Ask and answer.**

What have we got at nine o'clock on Tuesdays?

We've got maths.

What time is the break?

It's at half past ten.

School subjects

DIVERSICUS

🎧 2.32

1 Should we do our project on geography, history or art?

We should do all three.

Then we should go out and do research.

2 Hi, Ivan. We need to go out and get some information. Can you come with us?

Yes, of course. But you should ask your parents first.

3 Mum, can we go out for the day with Ivan?

Yes, of course. I can't come. I should practise for the show.

And I have to cook. Sorry!

4 Wow. This is one of the most famous markets in the world.

First it was made of wood, but now it's made of stone.

5 It's late. I have to get information about water sports for my project, too. I think we should go to the sea now.

Yes, come on!

6 Look. You can go fishing, sailing and windsurfing here.

Ivan, be careful. We shouldn't go so fast.

7 Ben, Kim! What a nice surprise!

Mum, Dad, what are you doing here at the beach?

8 We worked really hard and we finished quickly. Now it's our break.

It's beautiful here. We should all stay for lunch.

1 🎧 2.33 **Listen. Who says it?**

Story: *should/shouldn't* in context

Language practice 1

1 Look at the picture. Are the children interested in this subject?

2 Read. Complete the text with *should* or *shouldn't*.

To do well at school you ¹should arrive at your classroom at the right time. You ² __ have your books, notebook and pencil and you ³ __ always listen carefully to your teacher. You ⁴ __ eat in class and you ⁵ __ talk to your classmates when the teacher's giving the lesson. You ⁶ __ put your feet on the desks or the chairs, and you ⁷ __ pass notes during class time. You ⁸ __ do your homework and projects as well as you can and you ⁹ __ study hard. You ¹⁰ __ copy in exams. You ¹¹ __ have fun during your break.

Grammar spotlight

You **should** listen to your teacher.
You **shouldn't** talk when your teacher's giving the lesson.
Should you copy in exams?   No, you **shouldn't.**

3 Read and write four sentences.

Paul goes to bed late. It's difficult for him to study at school. What should he do? What shouldn't he do?

_____
_____
_____

mission STAGE 1

Describe how to be good at a subject.

- Choose a subject. Write three things you should do and three things you shouldn't do to learn this subject well.
- Find other people in the class who chose the same subject and make a group.
- Compare your lists and create one list with the five best ideas.

In geography, you should read maps.

You shouldn't copy information from the Internet.

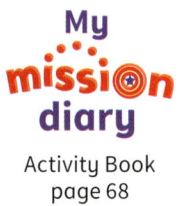

My mission diary
Activity Book page 68

should/shouldn't

Vocabulary 2 and song

1 🎧 2.35 ▶ **Listen and match. Then sing the song.**

I've got a **laptop**,
With some great **apps**.
It's got an **e-book** and wifi
And a special **rucksack**.

There's an online **dictionary**
To see what words mean.
There's no **bin** in my room,
It's there on the screen.

**I can do it all …
On my brilliant laptop.**

I do my homework.
I use the **Internet**.
I find safe **websites**
On the World Wide Web.

I can copy and cut,
Paste a photo or two.
I don't need **scissors**
And I don't need **glue**.
Chorus

2 🎧 2.37 📝 **Listen. Write the words.**

3 **Play the game. Ask and answer. Then tell the class.**

Find someone who …
1. reads e-books
2. has got a laptop
3. has got a rucksack
4. plays computer games
5. uses a dictionary
6. doesn't use the Internet to do homework

Do you read e-books?

No, I don't.

Peter doesn't read e-books.

Let's talk about homework. What do you use to do your homework?

72 Extension of school vocabulary

Language practice 2

1 Look at the picture. What do you think the boy is good at?

2 🎧 2.38 Listen and answer the questions.

1. What's David's favourite subject?
   _____

2. What's he good at?
   _____

3. What isn't he good at?
   _____

3 What are your friends good at? Ask and answer with five friends.

> Christina, what are you good at?

> I'm good at taking photos.

> Are you good at music?

> No, I'm not very good at music.

⭐ 🎧 2.39 Grammar spotlight

I**'m good at** maths.
Are you **good at** sport?
I**'m** not very **good at** drawing.

4 Write about what your friends are good at.

Cristina's good at taking photos.
_____
_____
_____

mission STAGE 2

Find out what your classmates are good at.
- In your groups, share your notes from Activities 3 and 4.
- Ask and answer to find out what every person in the class is good at.

> What is Sara good at?

> She's good at football.

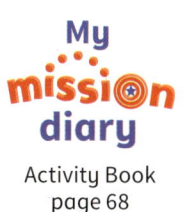

My mission diary
Activity Book page 68

be good at + noun/gerund 73

Cross-curricular

Where are we?

1 Watch the video.

2 🎧 2.40 Listen and read. Then look at the maps and match.

> political map   physical map   street map

In geography, we learn about maps. We need maps to find places and show distances between places.

There are different types of maps, including:

a **political maps**, which show borders between countries or between areas inside a country;

b **street maps**, which show the different roads in an area;

c **physical maps**, which show natural features in an area, like rivers, mountains and lakes.

3 🎧 2.41 Listen and read the information about maps. Answer the questions.

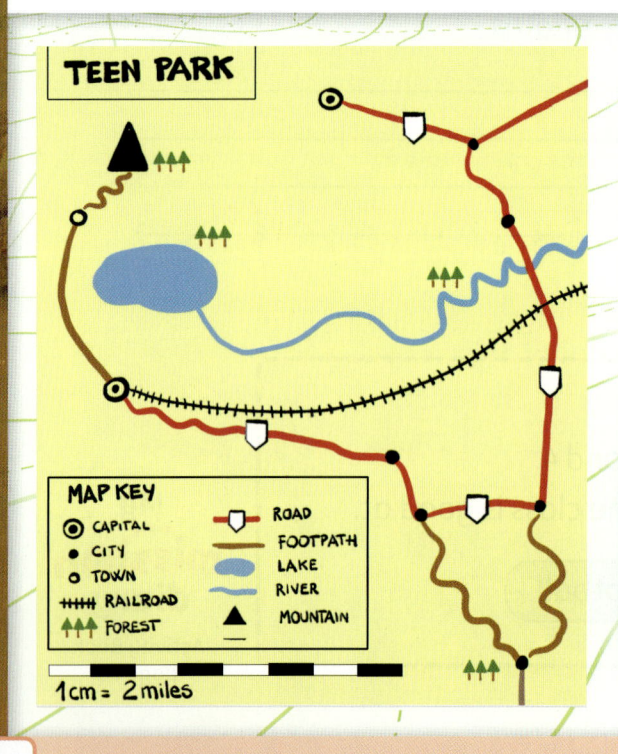

Maps

All maps have a **title** which tells us the name of the place on the map.

The **scale** shows the real distance between two places.

The pictures on a map are called **symbols**. They represent real things, like mountains or buildings.

The **key** explains what each symbol or colour means.

1 Find these things on the map: a river, a mountain, a lake and a forest.

2 What is the scale of the map?

3 How far is it from the forest to the lake? Use a ruler to find out.

TEEN PARK

MAP KEY
- ◉ CAPITAL
- • CITY
- ○ TOWN
- ┼┼┼┼ RAILROAD
- ▲▲▲ FOREST
- ⛳ ROAD
- ━━ FOOTPATH
- ～ LAKE
- ～ RIVER
- ▲ MOUNTAIN

1cm = 2 miles

74 Learn about maps and symbols

Culture

4 🎧 2.42 **Listen and read. Where is Cappadocia?**

Cappadocia, Turkey, is different from any other place on Earth. It is a very high area: over 1,000 metres above the sea. There are many mountains across this area which are thousands of years old and made from volcanic rock. Some of these mountains are really high, like Kayseri, which is the highest at 3,916 metres!

Because Cappadocia is so high, the weather can change a lot. It can be very hot some days and very cold other days.

The people who lived in Cappadocia many years ago made small houses inside the mountains and rocks. You should visit it because you can explore inside the exciting houses and see how the people lived!

5 Read the text again and complete the fact file.

FACT FILE: Cappadocia	
Where is it? _____	Why should you visit? _____
How high is it above the sea? _____	What's the highest mountain? _____
What's the weather like? _____	Where did the people live? _____

6 Discuss with a partner. What famous natural features are there in your country?

> The Pyrenees are a mountain range in Spain.

mission STAGE 3

Make a prize for each subject or activity.
- In your groups, think of a prize for each subject or activity in your Stage 2 notes.
- Design your prizes.

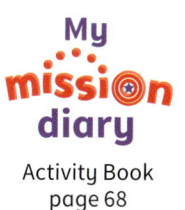

My mission diary
Activity Book page 68

Learn about Cappadocia in Turkey 75

Literature

1 Look at the pictures. What do you think the legend in this story is about? Make predictions.

2 Now read and listen to the story and check your predictions.

🎧 2.43 THE PROJECT

Katy, Mike and Harold were in the library talking about a project about Turkey. Mr Carlton, their teacher, said they could choose any topic for their project, but it should be about Turkey.

'Betty's group is doing their project about the geography of Turkey,' said Katy.

Harold was reading about Turkey on a website. 'The history of Turkey is very interesting. It was part of the Ottoman Empire!'

'Freddy's group's doing their project about that,' said Katy. 'What about science?'

'No,' said Harold. He didn't like science.

Katy looked at her timetable. 'The project's for Friday,' she said. 'Let's hurry up!' Katy had an idea. 'Our project can be about Turkish literature. I'm sure that Turkey has lots of stories and myths. These can teach us a lot about a place.'

'Great idea! We should find one on the Internet. Mr Carlton likes us to use IT,' said Mike.

'Why don't we do something original, like re-write the story as a poem? I'm good at writing poems,' said Katy. 'Mike's good at art. He can draw the pictures. And you're good at acting, Harold. You can read it to the class!'

'Perfect,' said Mike. So that's what they did!

Text type: A narration and poem

THE MOUSE AND THE CAMEL

A mouse came out of his hole in the ground,
Into the sunlight, and looked around.
He saw that a camel was walking by,
With rope around it. The mouse didn't know why.
So he took the rope, and feeling happy,
He pulled the camel along, singing loudly!

But soon they came to a river wide,
And the mouse felt sick and strange inside.
'Oh please, Mr Camel, please help me,
I don't like water, as you can see!'
So the camel told the mouse to jump
Onto his back, and sit on his hump.

But when they got to the other side,
He said 'Get off! That's the end of your ride!
And understand, you silly little thing,
That in the desert the camel is king!'

Their project was a great success. Everyone loved it!

3 **Work in groups. Use the words in the box to help you retell the story.**

> project teacher geography history idea mouse
> camel rope desert river back king success

4 **The project was a success because Katy, Mike and Harold worked together in a team. When do you work in teams? Do you like working in a team?**

Social and emotional skill: Team work and respecting the ideas of others

A2 Flyers

1 **Look at the picture. Ask and answer.**

1 Where are the children?
2 Count the boys.
3 Which names are boys' names?
4 Where is the teacher?
5 Count the girls.
6 Which names are girls' names?

George **Richard** **Megan**

Sophia **David** **Robert** **Katy**

2 **Point to a person in the picture and ask your partner to describe him/her.**

3 **Listen and find the person. Say his/her name.**

Richard

There are five questions but six names, so one name is extra.

Preparation for Listening Part 1

Review

mission in action!

6

Give prizes to your classmates.

- ★ In your groups, give your prizes to your classmates in the other groups.
- ★ Tell them why you're giving them the prize.
- ★ Tell them what the prize is.
- ★ Remember to say thank you when you get your prize!

You are good at English.

Your prize is a book.

My mission diary
Activity Book page 68

Can you remember?

1. Which was Pablo's favourite day? Why?
2. Where did Jim, Jenny and their friends go after the market?
3. Say three things you should do to do well in school.
4. What's David good at?
5. Say three types of maps.
6. Who's good at writing poems: Katy, Mike or Harold?

Unit consolidation

Review • • • Units 4–6

1 ▶ **Watch the video and do the quiz.**

2 🎧 2.45 **Listen and choose.**

1. My cousin eats very *quickly* / *slowly*. She should eat more *quickly* / *slowly* as she always gets a stomach-ache!

2. My brother *isn't* / *is* good at skating. He does it very *badly* / *well*! He should practise more.

3. My sister isn't good at fishing. She should do it more *quietly* / *loudly* as she's too *loud* / *quiet*!

4. I'm learning to sail so I do it very *carefully* / *loudly*.

5. I can kick a ball very *hard* / *fast*.

3 **Talk to your partner about one of the words below, but don't say the word. Can your partner guess it?**

art  maths  history  geography  scissors

e-book  dictionary  bin  website 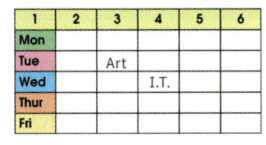 subject

> You work with numbers. — Maths!

80 Consolidation of units 4–6

4 Read the text. Then write *yes* or *no*. Correct the sentences that are wrong.

> We went to the theatre last night to watch the play *The Jungle Book*. The stage was so beautiful. There was a big jungle with a dark blue sky. There was a gold star and a bright moon in the sky. They were made of paper. On one side there was a light-blue waterfall made of soft material. On the other side there were four plants, two gold and two green. They were made of rubber. There were two small birds on the plants. One of the birds had spotted wings. They were made of wool! It was very clever.

1. There was an island on the stage.
   No. There was a jungle on the stage.

2. There was a dark blue sky.
   _____

3. There were two silver stars in the sky.
   _____

4. There was a bright moon.
   _____

5. There was a waterfall.
   _____

6. There were three gold plants.
   _____

7. The two birds had spotted wings.
   _____

5 Read the text again and draw the set.

6 Find these objects in your house. Complete the table. Write.

	How many are there?	What are they made of?
chair		
desk		
door		
window		
book		

I have nine chairs in my house. Three are made of plastic, six are made of wood.

Consolidation of units 4–6

7 When I grow up ...

1 ▶ **Watch the video. Ask and answer.**

What jobs do people in your family do?
Would you like to do these jobs? Why/why not?

mission Choose your dream job

In this unit I will:

1. Compare different jobs.
2. Add personality descriptions to each job.
3. Discuss the everyday tasks of a job.
★ Go to a job fair.

Vocabulary 1

1 🎧 3.02 **Listen. Why are these people talking to the children?**

Diversicus is in Spain. Today some people are at the circus to talk to the children for the newspaper The Daily Press.

waiter — actor — cook — driver — journalist — photographer — artist — designer — singer

2 🎧 3.03 ▶ **Say the chant.**

3 🎧 3.04 **Listen again and complete.**

> photographer   artist   driver   singer   designers   cook   journalist   acrobat

1. Betty Parks is a ___.
2. Oliver's a ___.
3. Su-Lin's mum's a ___.
4. Su-Lin's grandparents are ___ and ___.
5. Jenny's dad's a ___.
6. Pablo's uncle's an ___ and a ___.

Jobs 83

DIVERSICUS 🎧 3.05 ▶

1
— We've got our dance class today.
— And our tour of the city centre.
— Hi, kids. Are you ready? Shall we go now?

2
— Here's your lunch.
— Thanks, Ben.
— We can eat it in the park and if the weather's good, there are boat rides.

3 *Later ...*
— Our Spanish dance lesson is at 11.30.
— When we finish our tour, can you take us to this address, please?
— Yes, I can. No problem.

4
— Hello, only me! Can I come, too?
— Yes, of course.

5
— OK, follow me. When you dance, you look in the mirror.
— It helps you to dance better if you look in the mirror.

6
— Can we go on the boat ride now?
— Yes, and look! If we get the tickets online, we don't have to wait to buy them there.

7
— Look! There's a funfair!
— That's right, Jim. We've got four hours, then we have to go home.
— Brilliant!

8 *Later ...*
— If we buy this photo, we can always remember our perfect day.
— Yes! It was a perfect day. Thank you, Miguel and Lily.

1 🎧 3.06 **Listen and say *yes* or *no*.**

Story: *when* and *if* clauses in context

Language practice 1

1 Look at the picture. What's the boy doing?

2 Read and answer.

William's good at art and he loves taking photos. He wants to be a photographer when he grows up. Last year he joined a club for young photographers. Every year they have a competition for the best photo, and if you win, you get a big prize. If William wins, he wants to buy a fantastic new camera so he can take much better photos. If he doesn't win the competition, he hopes to get a new camera for his birthday.

1 What does William want to be when he grows up?
 He wants to be a photographer when he grows up.

2 What do you get if you win the competition?
 _____

3 What does William want to buy if he wins?
 _____

4 What does he hope to get if he doesn't win the competition?
 _____

🎧 3.07 Grammar spotlight

When you **dance**, you **look** in the mirror.
If you **win**, you **get** a big prize.
If William **wins**, he **wants** to buy a fantastic new camera.

3 Answer the questions. What do you do if …

1 you've got a cold? _____
2 you haven't got a pen? _____
3 your homework is difficult? _____
4 the waiter brings you the wrong food? _____

mission STAGE 1

Compare different jobs.

- Work with a partner. Choose three jobs you know.
- Individually, write a short description of each job. What do they do? Where do they work?
- Compare your descriptions with your partner.

> Waiters work in restaurants and cafés. When the customers finish their food, the waiter takes the plates.

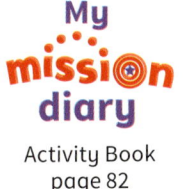

My mission diary
Activity Book page 82

Zero conditional 85

Vocabulary 2 and song

1 🎧 3.08 Listen and point. Say the names. Then sing the song.

I know a man.
Oh, yeah. What's he like? …
He's **interesting** and **kind**,
Interesting and **kind**.

I know a boy.
Oh, yeah. What's he like? …
He's **friendly** and **clever**,
Friendly and **clever**.

I know a dog.
Oh, yeah. What's it like? …
It's **lazy** and **lovely**,
Lazy and **lovely**.

I know a girl.
Oh, yeah. What's she like? …
She's **unkind** and **unfriendly**,
Unkind and **unfriendly**.

I know a woman.
Oh, yeah. What's she like? …
She's **popular** and **brave**,
Popular and **brave**.

Sophie

Dan

Harry

Rex

Emma

2 🎧 3.10 Listen and say the word.

3 Close the book. Ask and answer about the people in the song.

What's Sophie like? She's brave.

Who's lazy? Rex is lazy.

Let's talk about your family. Can you describe them?

86 Personality adjectives

Language practice 2

1 🎧 3.11 **Listen. Why is Frank's family in the newspaper?**

_____
_____

🎧 3.12 Grammar spotlight

What does your grandad **look like**?	He's very tall and he's got short, grey hair.
What**'s** your uncle **like**?	He's very friendly.

2 **Ask and answer about Frank's family.**

- What does Frank's uncle look like?
- He's got short dark hair and a beard.

3 **Ask your friends about their families.**

cousin   uncle   aunt   grandfather   grandmother   sister   brother   mum   dad

- What does your dad look like?
- He's got long brown hair and blue eyes.
- What's your brother like?
- He's lazy and kind.

mission STAGE 2

Add personality descriptions to each job.

- With your partner, discuss what personality each job needs.

  - What are teachers like?
  - I think teachers are friendly and clever.

- Write a personality description for each job.

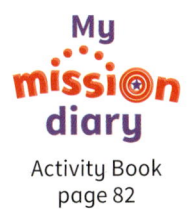

My mission diary
Activity Book page 82

look like, be like   87

Cross-curricular

Time detectives

1 Watch the video. Then read the text.

> Do you like investigating the past? You might like to be an archaeologist then! Archaeologists look for things that could give us information about how people lived in the past.

2 Talk to a partner about the pictures. Which pictures interest you? Why?

a b c d e f g h

3 Look at the pictures. What is the girl looking at in the museum? How old do you think the objects are?

4 What do these objects tell us about this time in history?

Learn about archaeology

Culture

5 🎧 3.13 **Listen and read Paula's story and answer the questions.**

Beautiful paintings

My dad is an archaeologist. Last year, he visited Spain. There is lots of work for an archaeologist in Spain because it's got many examples of how people lived in the past. Its history is very old! My dad went to the Altamira Caves. The caves are famous because archaeologists discovered the first cave paintings there in 1895. My dad says that in the past, people told stories using art. They didn't write like we do.

Bison, Altamira Caves, Santander, Spain

The paintings are over 14,000 years old. Many of the paintings on the cave walls show animals and people hunting. In one cave, a really big painting showed a bison (a type of animal). We think the paintings tell the story of how people hunted.

There were no paints or paintbrushes then so the cave people used the things they found around them. They used sticks, leaves and animal hair for their brushes. They made paint with fruits, plants and blood!

When I grow up I want to be an archaeologist like my father. He has a very interesting job and he sees amazing things!

Paula White

1 What job does Paula's father do? _____
2 Where did he go to visit the caves? _____
3 Why did they paint on the walls of the caves? _____
4 What did the early cave people paint pictures of? _____
5 How did they make their paint? _____

6 📒 **Make your own 'cave painting' to show how life is today.**

mission STAGE 3

Discuss the everyday tasks of a job.
- With your partner, choose one of your jobs.
- Individually, make a list of all the tasks someone with that job does.
- Compare your list with your partner.

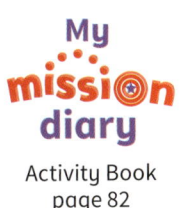

My mission diary
Activity Book page 82

Learn about the Altamira Caves in Spain   89

Literature

1 Work in small groups. Talk about when people are brave. Do you know anyone who is brave?

2 Look at the pictures. Who do you think is brave? Read and check.

DON QUIXOTE, SANCHO AND THE WINDMILLS

Narrator: A long time ago in Spain in a land called La Mancha, there was a quiet village with a large house. The man who lived in the house was called Alonso Quijano. Alonso read books all day about brave knights. He read so much that sometimes he forgot to eat or sleep. He dreamed about saving women in danger and fighting dragons. One day he decided to become a knight and he changed his name to Don Quixote. He put on his grandfather's armour and he rode his horse Rocinante. He asked his good friend Sancho Panza to join him and he promised to pay him lots of money in return.
This story is about one of their fantastic adventures …

Quixote: Look, Sancho! Our next great adventure. Can you see them?
Sancho: What?
Quixote: Thirty or forty giants over there.
Sancho: What giants?
Quixote: Over there! Look how long their arms are. They're moving in all directions.
Sancho: Dear friend. You think they look like giants but they're windmills and the arms you can see are their sails blowing in the wind.

Text type: An adventure play script

Quixote: Be quiet, Sancho! And prepare my horse for me! If you are afraid, you can stay here.
Sancho: No, I'm not afraid. What I mean is …
Quixote: Let's go, Rocinante.

[Don Quixote and his horse ride quickly towards the windmills.]

Quixote: Don't run, unkind giants!

[The windmill catches Don Quixote and Rocinante and then throws them down.]

Sancho: Friend! Are you alright? I told you that …
Quixote: Be quiet, Sancho! Someone changed the giants into windmills. It's magic!
Sancho: Yes, yes, my friend. Let me help you.
Narrator: And they continued on their journey to find their next adventure.

3 Work in groups of three. Act out the story.

A2 Flyers

1 Put the words in the right group.

head   beans   ~~actor~~   strawberry   photographer   badminton   skating
moustache   soup   finger   farmer   journalist   sailing   waiter

food	jobs	sports	body
	actor		

2 Look at the example. Which words help you to choose the answer?

This person uses a camera at work.   *a photographer*

3 Underline the words that help you in these sentences.

1. You have to remember a lot of words for this job and you work on a stage.   *an actor*
2. This is a popular job for people who can paint or draw very well.   *an artist*
3. This is a good job if you like food and you want to work in the kitchen at a restaurant.   *a cook*
4. There are lots of these at a concert for a singer and they are different colours.   *lights*
5. A person with this job uses a car and can work in a city or for a famous pop star!   *a driver*

4 Play the game.

Places: circus   school   zoo   museum   station

The home: hall   balcony   garden   bathroom   desk

This is where acrobats work.   The circus.

Copy the words carefully and spell them correctly too!

Preparation for Reading and Writing Part 1

Review

mission in action!

Go to a job fair.

- ⭐ Move around the classroom.
- ⭐ In pairs, ask and answer about your classmates' jobs.
- ⭐ Say what you think about the job.
- ⭐ Choose your favourite job.

What does an actor do?

I wouldn't like to be an actor. I'm not good at performing on stage.

My mission diary
Activity Book page 82

Can you remember?

1. Which Diversicus character's grandfather is an artist?
2. How did Miguel buy the tickets for the boat ride?
3. Why did William enter the photography competition?
4. What's the name of the lovely and lazy dog?
5. What does an archaeologist do?
6. What did Don Quixote think the windmills were?

Unit consolidation 93

8 City break

1 ▶ **Watch the video. Ask and answer.**

What do you like to do in the city?
Where's your favourite place in the city?

mission Create a guide to a town

In this unit I will:

1. Make a map of a town.
2. Ask and give directions.
3. Add some green spaces to the town.
★ Give a presentation about the town.

Vocabulary 1

1 🎧 3.15 **Listen. Who helps the Friendly family?**

Diversicus is in the USA. This evening the Friendly family are in their mobile home. They're lost.

left (←)
right (→)
straight on (↑)

North West East South

2 🎧 3.16 ▶ **Say the chant.**

3 🎧 3.17 **Listen and complete.**

left   river   lorry   right   ~~park~~   east   south

1 The Friendly family need to get to the lorry __park__ .
2 The lorry park is next to the _____ .
3 They are in the north, but they need to go _____ .
4 When they get to Road 95, they turn _____ .
5 On Road 95 they need to go _____ .
6 When they get to Road 9, they turn _____ .
7 Ivan is in Rose's _____ .

Directions

DIVERSICUS

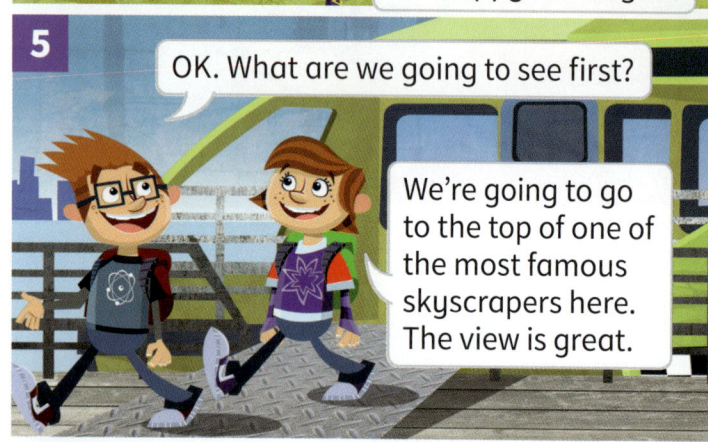

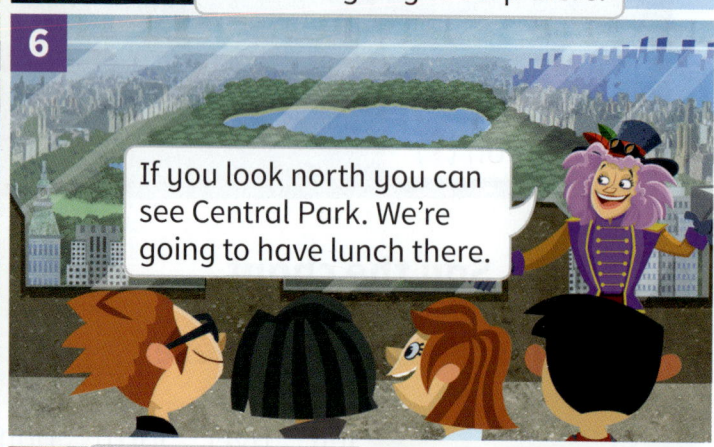

1 I'm going to take a water taxi to New York City tomorrow. Do you want to come?

Oh! Yes please!

2 *The next day ...* What's the weather like today? Is it going to rain?

I don't know, but I'm going to take my umbrella.

3 Jim, I don't think you're going to need an umbrella. It isn't going to rain.

I'm happy to carry it.

4 What's that? Are we going to stop there?

It's the Statue of Liberty. No, we aren't going to stop there.

5 OK. What are we going to see first?

We're going to go to the top of one of the most famous skyscrapers here. The view is great.

6 If you look north you can see Central Park. We're going to have lunch there.

7 Let's have our picnic here on the grass.

I don't know. I think it's going to rain.

8 Oh no! It's raining!

Here you are, Rose. Take my umbrella.

Thank you, Jim. You're very kind ... and I'm very wet.

1 Listen and say *yes* or *no*.

Story: *be going to* in context

Language practice 1

⭐ 🎧 3.20 Grammar spotlight

I'm **going to take** my umbrella.
It **isn't going to rain**.
What **are** we **going to see** first?

1 Look at the picture. What are the children learning to do?

_____

2 Read and complete the text with these words.

> isn't   ~~next~~   We're   On   it's   stay   going to

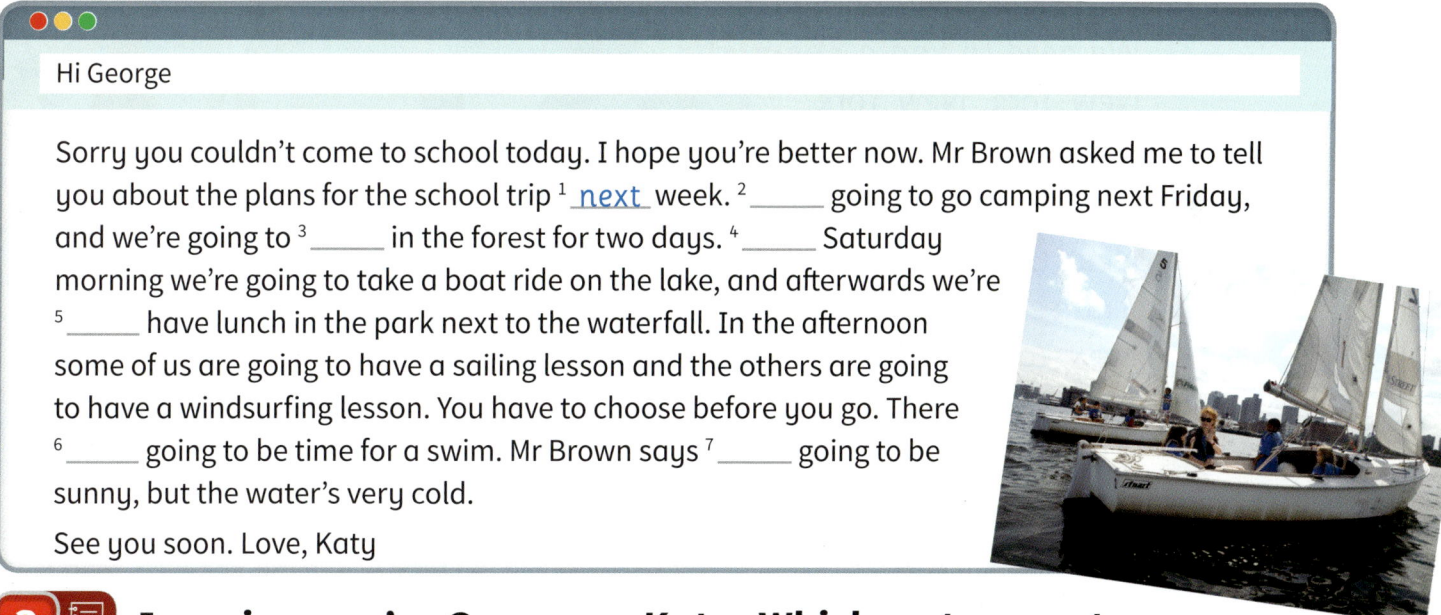

Hi George

Sorry you couldn't come to school today. I hope you're better now. Mr Brown asked me to tell you about the plans for the school trip ¹ _next_ week. ² _____ going to go camping next Friday, and we're going to ³ _____ in the forest for two days. ⁴ _____ Saturday morning we're going to take a boat ride on the lake, and afterwards we're ⁵ _____ have lunch in the park next to the waterfall. In the afternoon some of us are going to have a sailing lesson and the others are going to have a windsurfing lesson. You have to choose before you go. There ⁶ _____ going to be time for a swim. Mr Brown says ⁷ _____ going to be sunny, but the water's very cold.

See you soon. Love, Katy

3 Imagine you're George or Katy. Which water sport are you going to choose? Why? Write an email to Mr Brown.

mission STAGE 1

Make a map of a town.

- Work in small groups. Decide which places you're going to have in your town. Decide which materials you're going to use to make the map.

  > We're going to use cardboard for the sports centre.

- Make the buildings and label them, then label directions on the map.

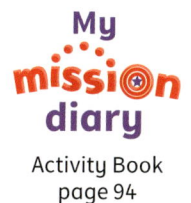

My mission diary
Activity Book page 94

Future with *be going to*   **97**

Vocabulary 2 and song

1 3.21 **Listen and match. Then sing the song.**

We're at the **airport**,
New York, JFK.
We're going to see the **buildings**,
New York, New York.

We're going to go to the **bank**,
To get some **money**.
Then to the **post office**,
To buy some **stamps**.
New York, New York.

We need a new toothbrush,
And some new toothpaste.
We need to find a **chemist's**.
New York, New York.

Let's go to a **theatre**,
Visit a **museum**,
Near the **university**,
And see some art.
New York, New York.

There's a brilliant **hotel**,
With a **restaurant**.
We're going to have a burger.
New York, New York.

2 **Imagine you're going to go to New York. What are you going to see? What are you going to do? Tell your partner.**

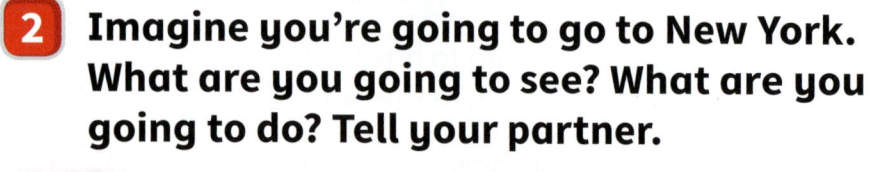

3 **Write an email to your friend about your plans in Activity 2.**

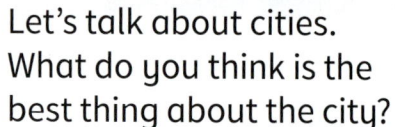

Let's talk about cities. What do you think is the best thing about the city?

98 Places in town

Language practice 2

1 🎧 3.23 **Listen and follow the directions on the map.**

> ⭐ 🎧 3.24 **Grammar spotlight**
>
> We should go **into** the park **through** North Gate.
>
> **across**, **into**, **out of**, **over**, **past**, **round**, **through**

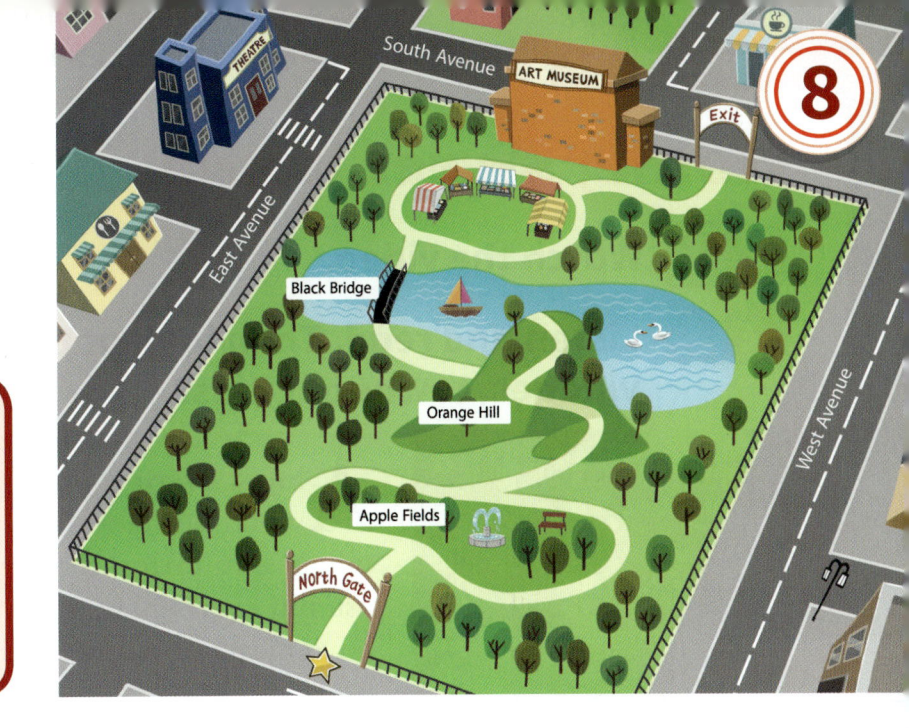

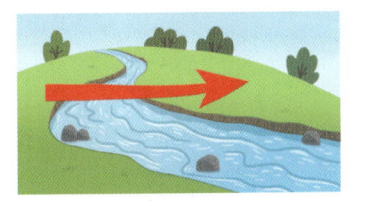

across

over

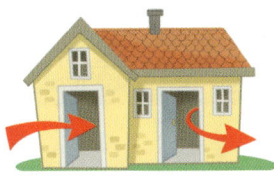

into   out of

through

round

past

2 **Look at the map. Give your partner directions from Black Bridge to the theatre.**

3 **Write directions from your house to the school.**

mission STAGE 2

Ask and give directions.
- Work with a partner.
- Use your map. Ask and give directions in your town.

> I am at the post office. How do I get to the hotel?

> Go across the bridge and past the museum. The hotel is on the right.

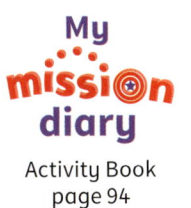

My mission diary
Activity Book page 94

Prepositions of movement 99

Cross-curricular

Home, sweet home

1 Watch the video.

2 🎧 3.25 Listen and read. Then look at the pictures. Which show villages, towns or cities?

Almost every country in the world has cities, towns and villages. In **cities**, the population is usually over 300,000 people. They have many buildings and roads.

Towns usually have over 1,000 people. They are smaller than cities and their roads are not as wide as city roads.

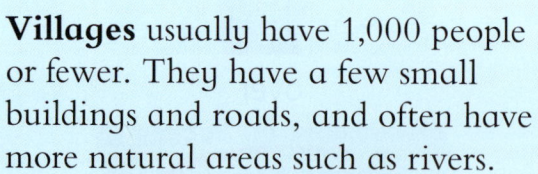

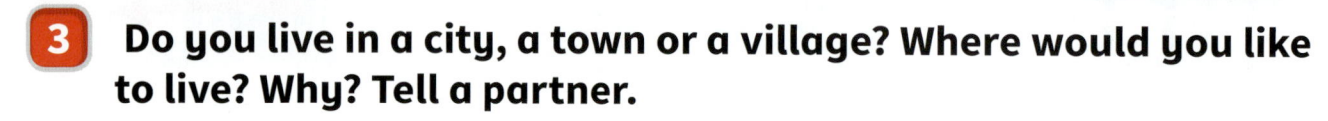

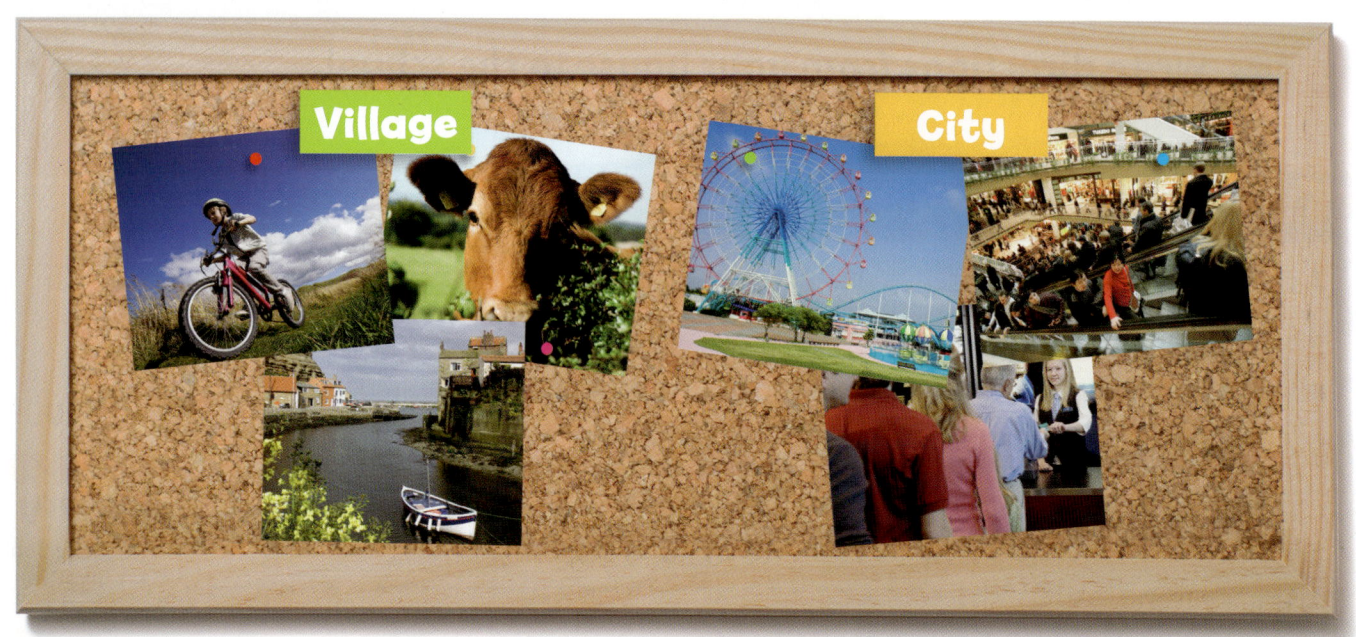

Villages usually have 1,000 people or fewer. They have a few small buildings and roads, and often have more natural areas such as rivers.

3 Do you live in a city, a town or a village? Where would you like to live? Why? Tell a partner.

4 Talk about the good and bad things about living in a village and living in a city. Use the photos to help you.

Village

City

100 Learn about cities, towns and villages

Culture

5 🎧 3.26 **Listen and read the fact file. Talk about how it is different from where you live.**

Fact file: New York City

Location	North-east coast of the USA. On the Atlantic Ocean.
Size	789 square kilometres
Population	Around 8.5 million people
Climate	Very hot in some parts of the year and very cold in others
City characteristics	City of skyscrapers – over 6,000 high-rise buildings. Very busy city. People from all over the world live here
Places of interest	Manhattan Times Square The Statue of Liberty The Museum of Modern Art Brooklyn Bridge Central Park The Empire State Building

6 ✏️ **Write a fact file about a city, town or village in your own country. Use the headings in Activity 5 to help you.**

mission — STAGE 3

Add some green spaces to your town.
- In groups, choose some green spaces to include in your town.
- Use symbols to add them to your map and create a key.

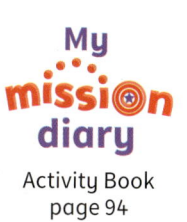

My mission diary
Activity Book page 94

Learn about New York City

Literature

1 Look at the pictures and answer the questions.
1 Where do you think the family are? _____
2 What do you think they're doing? _____
3 Are you good at giving directions? _____

🎧 3.27
THE ROAD TO HOPE

I'm Kay and he's Jay, and we're both here today,
To talk about our life in the USA.
Our country is big and our country is wide,
Over two thousand miles from side to side.

Last year we went on a trip in the car.
'Don't worry,' said Mum, 'we aren't going to go far.'
We wanted to visit this small town called Hope,
Where Grandma was born, she's called Sue-Ella Cope.

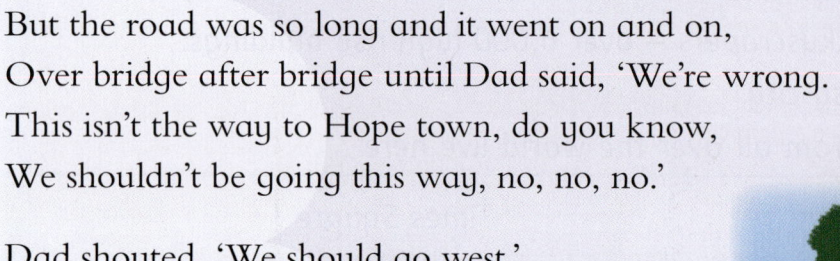

But the road was so long and it went on and on,
Over bridge after bridge until Dad said, 'We're wrong.
This isn't the way to Hope town, do you know,
We shouldn't be going this way, no, no, no.'

Dad shouted, 'We should go west.'
But Mum said, 'No, east is best.'
We sat in silence, and looked at Yvonne,
Who picked up the laptop and turned it on.

Text type: A poem

Our sister so small, so clever, so kind,
Searched her laptop and tried hard to find,
An app that would help us all get to the town.
'Go left,' she said now, 'and go up please, not down.'

We went left at the shops and straight on at the light.
The day was so warm and the sun was so bright.
'Look!' said Yvonne. 'Can you all see the sign?
I'm quite good at finding directions online.'

We laughed and we laughed and said, 'Well done, Yvonne,
We're here in the town, and we didn't go wrong.
From now on it's your job to show us the way.
Thank you for helping us get here today.'

2 **Choose the word to describe the family's emotions. Why do they feel this way?**

1. The family are going on a trip. Everyone is *bored* / *excited* / *tired*.
2. Mum and Dad don't know how to get to Hope. They're *happy* / *angry* / *surprised*.
3. Jay and Kay don't know how to get to Hope. They're *afraid* / *bored* / *happy*.
4. Yvonne knows how to get to Hope. She's *calm* / *worried* / *tired*.

Social and emotional skills: Managing own emotions

A2 Flyers

1 **Look at the pictures in Activity 2. Find and point to six things that are different.**

> In my picture, the waiter is putting a milkshake on the table but in your picture, the waiter is putting some cake on the table.

2 🎧 3.28 **Listen. Does the girl talk about the same differences as you?**

> Listen carefully and talk about six differences. Try to use full sentences.

104 Preparation for Speaking Part 1

Review

mission in action!

Give a presentation about your town.

- ★ Describe the buildings and their location in the town using the map.
- ★ Explain how to get to different places in the town.
- ★ Describe all the green spaces in the town.
- ★ As a class, vote to choose the best town.

My mission diary
Activity Book page 94

Can you remember?

1. Where did the Friendly family need to get to?
2. Where were Rose and the children when it started to rain?
3. Where can you buy some stamps?
4. Name three buildings you don't usually see in a village.
5. What's the population of New York City?
6. What did Yvonne use to find directions?

9 Let's travel!

1 ▶ **Watch the video. Ask and answer.**

Where did you go for your last holiday?
What did you do there?

mission: Organise a summer camp

In this unit I will:

1. Prepare a three-day timetable.
2. Describe the activities at the summer camp.
3. Pack a bag for the summer camp.
★ Write a review about the summer camp.

Vocabulary 1

1 🎧 3.29 **Listen. What's the hero called?**

Diversicus is in Mexico. This morning Pablo's showing his friends the comic book which he finished yesterday.

Our superhero is **alone** …

A **strange** man

His **horrible**, **little** dog

It's **noisy**.

It's got a **huge** mouth.

He's **lucky**. He's got his **excellent**, **special** shoes.

2 🎧 3.30 ▶ **Say the chant.**

3 🎧 3.31 **Listen and say *yes* or *no*.**

Adjectives 107

DIVERSICUS

1. This huge old city is called Teotihuacan. People started building it more than 2,000 years ago. Today we're going to walk round and look at the Pyramids.

2. *Later ...* What did you do today?

We drove north-east of Mexico City to see the Pyramids.

3. Tonight is our last show! What did you like most about the tour?

Good question. Let's think.

4. After we met Grandma's sister in China, we ate the fantastic noodles which she made for us. That was my favourite day.

5. The funniest time was when Ivan carried the girls quickly through the jungle. He ran really fast when Fred came out of the trees.

6. For me the most exciting day was in Spain. We sailed across the river on a boat before we went to the funfair.

7. My funniest day was in New York. Rose got really wet before I gave her my umbrella.

8. Are we going to go on tour again next year, Rose?

Yes, of course. We're going to have more exciting adventures next year.

Can I come, too?

1 Listen. Who says it?

Story: *before, after, when* clauses in context

Language practice 1

🎧 3.34 Grammar spotlight

Rose got really wet **before** I gave her my umbrella.

He ran really fast **when** Fred came out of the trees.

After we met Grandma's sister in China, we ate the fantastic noodles.

1 Look at the photos. What are the children doing?

2 Choose the words to complete the text.

Well, this is our last article for the school newspaper. Before we ¹*go* / *arrive* on holiday, we should remember some of the most exciting things from the last year.

Our first trip was to the funfair. After we ²*get off* / *got off* one of the rides, we ³*buy* / *bought* this amazing photo.

One of our favourite trips was when we ⁴*visited* / *visit* the fire station. ⁵*After* / *If* we ⁶*meet* / *met* the brave firefighters there, we put on their helmets. George ⁷*took* / *take* this photo.

Last month we ⁸*go* / *went* camping in the forest. We took a boat ride on the lake ⁹*when* / *before* we had a windsurfing lesson. It ¹⁰*was* / *is* brilliant.

See you next year!

George and Katy

3 Ask and answer. What did you do …

1. when you got home from school yesterday?
2. after you got up this morning
3. when you arrived at school this morning?
4. before you had dinner last night?

mission STAGE 1

Prepare a three-day timetable.

- In groups, discuss some ideas for activities for your summer camp.

  On day one, let's go hiking after breakfast.

  Great idea! And for lunch let's go to the place where they make the best pancakes.

- Write your three-day timetable.

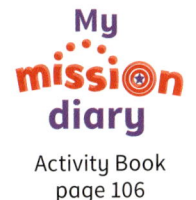

My mission diary
Activity Book page 106

before, after, when clauses

Vocabulary 2 and song

1 🎧 3.35 ▶ Listen and find the words from the song in the picture. Then sing the song.

This year's **tour** is over.
Yes, it is, we're on our way …
We're packing all our boxes
And the tent, the enormous **tent**.

I need to find my **pyjamas**
Before I pack my **trainers**.
I need to pack my **suitcase**,
Yes, I do. Yes, I do.

Chorus

After I pack my **rucksack**,
We're going to go on holiday.
We're going to go to the beach,
To make **sandcastles** by the sea.

Chorus

Don't forget to send these **postcards**,
With **views** of Mexico.
Remember to put the **stamp** on,
And take it to the post office.

Chorus

2 🎧 3.37 📝 Listen and write.

3 Imagine you're going to go on holiday next week. Ask and answer.

What are you going to pack in your suitcase?
I'm going to pack my trainers.
Why?
Because I'm going to play football.

Let's talk about holidays. What should people see and do when they are on holiday in your country?

On holiday

Language practice 2

1 🎧 3.38 **Listen. What's Sophia going to do on holiday? Say three things.**

⭐ 🎧 3.39 **Grammar spotlight**

You're going to be **tired** at the end of your holiday.

Yes, it is going to be **tiring**.

2 **What do you think about these things? Ask and answer.**

going to a museum   going to the beach   exams   jungles
camping   studying   shopping   computer games   football   dancing

boring   interesting   frightening   tiring   exciting   surprising

What do you think about going to a museum?

I think it's interesting.

3 **Tell your partner about the last time you were …**

1 bored
2 frightened
3 tired
4 excited
5 surprised
6 interested

The last time I was excited was when I went to a funfair.

mission STAGE 2

Describe the activities at the summer camp.

- In your groups, discuss the activities in your timetable.

  There's a walk on the beach and a sandcastle competition after the walk.

  That's going to be exciting!

- Write a short description for each activity.

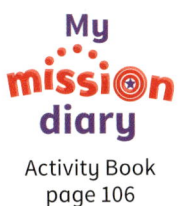

My mission diary

Activity Book page 106

-ed/-ing adjective endings   111

Cross-curricular

North, south, east and west

1 Watch the video.

2 Look at the pictures. What activities are the children doing?

3 Which activities do you think are exciting, frightening or tiring? What do you like doing in the countryside?

4 What should you take with you when you go hiking? Why? Choose and tell a partner.

> When you go hiking, you should take a map so you don't get lost.

112 Learn about what to take on a hiking trip

Culture

5 Look at the pictures. How can the sky help you find your way if you haven't got a compass?

6 🎧 3.40 Listen and read Jasmin's diary. What did they use to find their way? _____

Saturday July 15th

Day five in Mexico! Today was very interesting. We went to visit a pyramid at the top of the Tepozteco Mountain in Morelos. It was a beautiful walk. We went past waterfalls and amazing rainforests! We walked very far because the pyramid is very high up the mountain. On the way, we saw lots of lizards. We rested at the top of the mountain and we had a picnic. The view was lovely; we could look down on the beautiful town of Tepoztlan. Danny took lots of pictures.

When we were preparing to go back down the mountain, disaster happened! Danny fell and our compass broke. Oh no! How could we find our way with no compass?

We couldn't look at the stars because it was day time. Danny wanted to make a compass but we didn't have the right materials. Then Mum found the solution. The sun was getting lower in the sky. Of course! The sun rises in the east and it sets in the west. Now we knew where west was and it was easy to find south.

We arrived back at the hotel hot and dirty, but safe. Mum is now the superhero of the family. What's going to happen to us tomorrow?

7 Read the diary again and answer the questions.

1 Which country is Jasmin visiting?

2 What's the name of the mountain which they climbed?

3 What was at the top of the mountain?

4 What happened to the compass?

5 Why didn't they use the stars to find their way?

6 Why didn't they make a compass?

mission STAGE 3

Pack a bag for the summer camp.

- In your groups, discuss what items you're going to need for each activity.

> For hiking, we're going to need a compass and some boots.

> For visiting the town hall, we're going to need a camera and some money.

- Write a final list of things to pack for the summer camp.

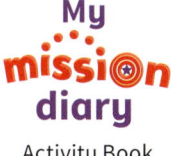

My mission diary
Activity Book page 106

Learn about a hiking trip in Mexico

Literature

1 What do these words mean? Discuss with a partner. Use the pictures or a dictionary to help you.

> volcano   shape   tent   warrior   tribe   broken heart

2 What's the story about? Make predictions. Then read and check.

🎧 3.41 **THE STORY OF POPOCATEPETL AND IZTACCIHUATL**

Harry and Sophie were on holiday in Mexico with their cousins, Jaime and Alicia. Before they went home, they wanted to climb Popocatepetl. Popocatepetl is a volcano not very far from Mexico City. The night before the climb, they camped at the bottom of the volcano with their mountain climbing guide. Harry and Jaime looked up at the volcano covered with snow.

'It's going to be exciting tomorrow,' said Jaime. Harry was excited, too.

'What a strange shape that other mountain is,' said Sophie suddenly. 'It looks like a woman lying down.'

The guide looked where she was pointing. 'Yes,' he said. 'It does. That's a volcano, too. Let's put up the tents before it gets dark, and then I can tell you the story of the two volcanoes.'

After they put up the tents, they all sat down and they listened to the story of Popocatepetl and Iztaccihuatl. It was very interesting.

114   Text type: A narration and legend

'Long ago, there was a beautiful princess called Iztaccihuatl. Popocatepetl was a young warrior. He was in love with the beautiful princess and she was in love with him. But before they could get married, another dangerous tribe attacked their tribe. The leader of Popocatepetl's tribe spoke to him. "We need you to help our tribe before you marry my daughter," he said. Popocatepetl had to say goodbye to Iztaccihuatl, and go and fight.

'Iztaccihuatl was lonely and sad. One day she heard that Popocatepetl was dead. She became very ill. In the end, she died of a broken heart.

'But Popocatepetl wasn't dead. Very soon, he returned. When he discovered that Iztaccihuatl was dead, he picked up her body in his arms and carried her away. He laid her down on the ground in a quiet place, and sat down next to her. Snow fell and covered their two bodies.'

The guide stopped and pointed up at the two mountains in front of them. 'Look! Popocatepetl and Iztaccihuatl are still there! They are the two volcanoes.'

3 **Choose the correct sentence. Discuss your choice with a partner.**

☐ The story of Popocatepetl and Iztaccihuatl is a true story.

☐ The story of Popocatepetl and Iztaccihuatl is a legend.

4 **Play the game.**

Think of a true story or a legend. Tell the story to a partner. Your partner guesses if your story is a true story or a legend.

Social and emotional skills: Showing respect for other cultures

A2 Flyers

1 **Look at the pictures in Activity 2. Answer the questions.**

Who's on holiday?   Where are they?

2 **Read the words. Match them with picture a, b or c.**

Nouns: suitcase   tent   boy   fire   rucksack
parents   bedroom   Mum   Frank   eggs

Verbs: Hurry up!   camp   cook   pack   laugh   talk

Adjectives: late   friendly   bored   cloudy   happy

Picture a: bedroom, hurry up!, pack …

3 **Choose some of the words and finish these sentences.**

Write between 20 and 30 words – you don't need to write more.

Picture a: Frank _____
Picture b: Mum _____
Picture c: When they arrived, _____
In the evening _____

116   Preparation for Reading and Writing Part 7

Review

mission in action!

9

Write a review about the summer camp.

- ★ Write the best thing about the summer camp.
- ★ Write the worst thing about the summer camp.
- ★ Present your summer camp and review.

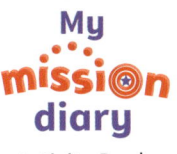

My mission diary
Activity Book page 106

"The hiking trip was the worst. We got lost and it was frightening."

"The horse-riding activity was the best. It was really amazing to see the sea from the top of the mountain."

Can you remember?

1. How did Pablo's superhero catch the strange man?
2. Whose favourite day was the trip to the funfair?
3. What did George and Katy do before their windsurfing lesson?
4. Which Diversicus character couldn't find his pyjamas?
5. Name five things you should take when you go hiking.
6. Who was Popocatepetl?

Unit consolidation

Review ... Units 7–9

1 Watch the video and do the quiz.

2 🎧 3.42 Listen to George and Helen and name the buildings on the map.

3 Work with a partner. Say which word is different and why.

1	brave	friendly	**unkind**
2	restaurant	chemist's	waiter
3	excellent	brilliant	horrible
4	pleasing	interesting	excited
5	money	post office	bank
6	driver	singer	dancer
7	tent	suitcase	hotel
8	north	straight on	east
9	huge	little	lazy
10	popular	unfriendly	lucky

> Number 1. Unkind is different because brave and friendly are positive and unkind is negative.

4 Choose five words from Activity 3 to talk about people you know.

> My cousin is a firefighter and she's very brave.

118 Consolidation of units 7–9

5 Read and complete the letter.

> tour pleased when bored hotel ~~excited~~ worried
> suitcase come worried interesting when

Hi William!

How are you? I was so happy to hear from you.

I'm so ¹ excited ! I'm going to go to the beach with my family tomorrow! We wanted to go camping but ² ___ my brother said he was ³ ___ about sleeping in a tent, my parents said we could go to a ⁴ ___ . My parents are ⁵ ___ because my rucksack is packed! But they are ⁶ ___ because my sister's ⁷ ___ is huge!

⁸ ___ we arrive, we're going to go on a ⁹ ___ of the museum. I think museums are ¹⁰ ___ but my brother always feels ¹¹ ___ . He wants to build sandcastles.

Where are you going to go on your holiday? If you ¹² ___ to my country, please write and tell me.

Love, Nicola

6 Write a reply to Nicola.

- Where am I going to go on holiday?
- Who am I going to go with?
- What are we going to do?
- How do we feel?

Consolidation of units 7–9   119

Grammar reference

Unit 1

Review question words: how, what, when, where, which, who, why

- We use *which*, *how*, *what*, *when*, *where*, *who* and *why* to ask questions. We use them to get information, we don't answer with 'yes' or 'no'.

Which acrobat is practising now? →	**Ivan** is practising now.
How are you today? →	I'm **very well**, thank you.
What is she doing? →	She's **having lunch**.
When does he have dinner? →	He has dinner **at half past six**.
Where is the school? →	It's **next to the park**.
Why are we getting up early today? →	**Because** school starts at seven o'clock.
Who are they talking to? →	They're talking to **the teacher**.

Remember:
I am = I'm   It is = It's   He is = He's   She is = She's
We are = We're   You are = You're   They are = They're

> Which country are we in today?

Was/were + could

- We use *was/were* + *could* to talk about an ability in the past.

I / She / He	**could** / **couldn't**	say a few words when	I / she / he	**was**	two.

When	you / we / they	**were** three,	you / we / they	**could** / **couldn't**	ride a bike.

Could	I / she / he	play the guitar when	I / she / he	**was**	four?
	you / we / they		you / we / they	**were**	

Yes,	I / she / he / you / we / they	could.

No,	I / she / he / you / we / they	couldn't.

> Could you do a handstand when you were four?

Defining relative clauses

- We use defining relative clauses to give important information about something.
  - We use *who* when we are talking about **a person**.
  - We use *which* when we are talking about **a thing**.
  - We use *where* when we are talking about **a place**.

	teacher	who	I like best.
That's the	car	which	my dad wants to buy.
	park	where	we play football.

> This is the town where I lived when I was a child.

Remember:
That is = That's

Past simple + *when*

- We use *when* and the past simple to talk about two things that happened close together in the past.

+	When we **saw** our friends,	→	we **told** them about our day.
?	When you **saw** your friends,	→	**did you tell** them about your day?
+	We **told** our friends about our day	→	when we **saw** them.
?	**Did** you **tell** your friends about your day	→	when you **saw** them?
?	What **did** they **do**	→	when they **got** home yesterday?

Remember:
(present) What does/do …? = (past) What did …?
(present) Do you …? = (past) Did you …?

> When we finished lunch, we went to the Great Wall of China.

Review of comparative and superlative adjectives, *as … as*:

- We use the **comparative** to talk about how two things compare.
  Mrs Friendly is **taller than** Su-Lin.
- We use the **superlative** to say something has more than the rest of the group.
  Ivan is **the tallest** person in Diversicus.
- Another way to make a comparison is using **not as … as**.
  Mrs Friendly and Su-Lin **aren't as tall as** Ivan.
- We use *as … as* to say that two things are the same.
  Ivan is **as tall as** a tree!

Remember:
We use *-er/-est* with short adjectives, e.g. *small = smaller/smallest*.
We use *more/the most* with long adjectives, e.g. *dangerous = more/the most dangerous*.

want/need + infinitive

- We use *want* to say when we would like something. We use *need* to give advice.

I You We They	want	
	don't want	**to go** to the park.
He She	wants	
	doesn't want	

I You We They	need	
	don't need	**to drink** a glass of water.
He She	needs	
	needs	

Do	I you we they	need want	**to get** some sleep?
Does	she he		

Do you want to go to school tomorrow? Then you need to get some rest!

Remember:
do not = don't
does not = doesn't

Unit 4

Adverbs

- We use adverbs to describe how something happens or how someone does something.

	Adjective	Adverb
add -ly	slow	Walk **slowly** in the classroom.
	careful	Listen **carefully** to the teacher.
	quiet	Work together **quietly**, please.
	quick	Finish your lunch **quickly**.
	bad	You don't draw **badly**!
	loud	Don't speak **loudly**, please.
	beautiful	He sings **beautifully**.
change -y to -i, add -ly	easy	I can do this homework **easily**.
irregular	good	You can play football very **well**!
stay the same	fast	She can run **fast**.
	hard	Look **hard** at the sentence. Can you see the mistake?

Run quickly! There's a bear behind us!

Grammar reference

Comparative adverbs

- We can make comparisons of actions using adverbs. We use comparative adverbs when we want to compare how something is done.

My sister swims	faster / more quickly	than me.

I can move more quietly than an elephant!

Be made of

- We use *be made of* to say what material something is.

It	is / isn't	made of wood.
They	are / aren't	

Is	it	made of wood?
Are	they	made of wood?

Yes,	it **is**. / they **are**.
No,	it **isn't**. / they **aren't**.

This scarf is made of wool.

Remember:
is not = isn't
are not = aren't

shall, could and let's for suggestions

- We use *shall*, *could* and *let's* to make suggestions.

Shall	we / I	make an acrobat costume?

We could	use card for the hats.
Let's	make masks for the theatre workshop?

Let's dress up like pirates! Arr!

Grammar reference

Unit 6

should/shouldn't

- We use *should* and *shouldn't* to give advice. We use *should* to talk about things which are a good idea. We use *shouldn't* to talk about things which are a bad idea.

I You He She We They	**should do** the homework.
	shouldn't be late for school.

Should	I you he she we they	**go** to the beach?

Yes,	I you he she we they	**should.**
No,		**shouldn't.**

> We should go out and do research for our project.

be good at + noun, be good at + gerund

- We use *be good at* when we want to say what subject or activity a person does well.

+	Lily is very **good at football**.
–	We aren't very **good at skipping**.
?	Are you **good at running** and **climbing**?
?	What **are** they **good at**?

> She's good at sports!

> He's good at science!

Unit 7

when and if clauses (zero conditionals)

- We use *when* and *if* clauses to talk about results which are always true.

if/when + present simple	**present simple**
If you **want** to learn to dance,	you **can** do classes after school.
When the weather **is** cold,	I **wear** my warm coat.

Present simple	**if/when + present simple**
We **don't play** football	**if** it's raining.
Emma **does** her homework before dinner	**when** she **gets** home early.

> Look in the mirror when you dance.

124 Grammar reference

look like, be like

- We use *look like* to talk about a person's physical appearance.
- We use *be like* to talk about a person's personality.

| What does your sister **look like**? | → | She's tall with dark hair. |
| What**'s** your sister **like**? | → | She's kind and friendly. |

What's your dog like?

It's lazy and lovely!

be going to

- We use *be going to* to talk about our plans for the future. We can also use it to make predictions.

+			
I	am		
She He	is	going to	go to the cinema.
You We They	are		

-			
I	am not		
She He	isn't	going to	listen to music.
You We They	aren't		

?			
Is	she he	going to	eat dinner?
Are	you we they		

+				-			
Yes,	she he	is.		No,	she he	isn't.	
	you we they	are.			you we they	aren't.	

Is it going to rain today?

Unit 8

Grammar reference 125

Prepositions of movement: *across, into, out of, over, past, round, through*

- We use prepositions of movement to talk about how someone or something moves.

Henry walked	across	the river.
Please come	into	the house.
Turn left when you go	out of	the door.
The bird flew	over	the building.
Every day I go	past	the bank.
We usually walk	round	the lake.
To get home, Lucy goes	through	the forest.

before, after, when clauses

- We can use *before, after* and *when* clauses to talk about when two things happened. *Before* means earlier and *after* means later. We use *when* to describe events happening at the same time.

Let's go to the museum	→	**before** we eat lunch.
Let's eat lunch	→	**after** we go to the museum.
Let's decide what to do next	→	**when** we're eating lunch.

> We ate the best noodles after we met Grandma's sister.

–ed / –ing adjective endings

- We use *-ed* adjectives to talk about how we feel.
- We use *-ing* adjectives to describe a person, thing or situation.

bor-	ing	This book is very **boring**.
	ed	I'm **bored** of reading this book.
interest-	ing	The film about Mexico was **interesting**.
	ed	Emily was **interested** in the film about Mexico.
tir-	ing	The walk to the waterfall was very **tiring**.
	ed	We were very **tired** when we arrived at the waterfall.

> This is very exciting! We aren't bored!

Unit 9

126 Grammar reference

Irregular verb list

Base form	Past simple
be	was
begin	began
bring	brought
build	built
buy	bought
can	could
catch	caught
choose	chose
come	came
do	did
drive	drove
eat	ate
fall	fell
feel	felt
find	found
fly	flew
forget	forgot
get	got
give	gave
go	went
grow	grew
have	had
hear	heard
hide	hid
hold	held
keep	kept

Base form	Past simple
learn	learnt
let	let
lose	lost
make	made
mean	meant
meet	met
must	must
put	put
ride	rode
run	ran
say	said
see	saw
send	sent
sit	sat
speak	spoke
stand	stood
swim	swam
take	took
teach	taught
tell	told
think	thought
throw	threw
wake	woke
wear	wore
write	wrote

Irregular verb list **127**